NETHERLANDS SCIENTIFIC COUNCIL FOR GOVERNMENT POLICY

Making Migration Work

THE FUTURE OF LABOUR MIGRATION IN THE EUROPEAN UNION

Jan Willem Holtslag, Monique Kremer and Erik Schrijvers (eds.)

Amsterdam University Press, Amsterdam 2013

Edited by: Netherlands Scientific Council for Government Policy / WRR

Cover and book design: cimon, The Hague
Cover illustration: hikrcn

ISBN   978 90 8964 557 9
e-ISBN 978 90 4851 951 4 (pdf)
e-ISBN 978 90 4851 952 1 (e-Pub)
NUR   741 / 763

Making Migration Work

This series consists of papers produced for the WRR that it regards as sufficiently significant and valuable to merit publication. The views and opinions expressed in these papers are those of the authors.

The WRR's offices are located at:
Lange Vijverberg 4-5
PO Box 20004
2500 EA The Hague, The Netherlands
Phone +31 (0)70 356 46 00
Fax +31 (0)70 356 46 85
E-mail info@wrr. nl
Website www.wrr.nl

CONTENTS

INTRODUCTION

The complexion of labour migration in the European Union (EU) has altered in recent years. Not only has there been a shift in the length of time labour migrants spend abroad, but the nature, scale and direction of the migration flows have also changed dramatically. The enlargements of the EU in 2004 and 2007 were influential in this respect. A growing economy and large wage gaps encouraged a large stream of workers to leave the new Member States for the old. The EU's open internal borders made it easy for them to return home or to move on to another Member State. This publication considers what this means for the future of labour migration and how policy should address this issue. For example, one possible implication is that the integration of newcomers will need to be viewed in a different light; unlike in the past, not all migrants are likely to remain in their destination country.

Another reason to consider the future of labour migration in the EU can be found in various demographic trends in the Member States, including the Netherlands. With their populations ageing and their birth rates declining, the labour force in these countries is also shrinking – a trend that is expected to lead to many new challenges, for example the affordability of the social welfare system and labour shortages when the baby boom generation retires. Some sectors are already feeling the pinch of these shortages. Labour migration – particularly of workers from outside the European Union – is thought to be one way to alleviate these shortages. But is it a realistic option?

The third reason concerns the sweeping changes that have taken place in employment relations since the labour migrant flows of the 1960s and 1970s, with flexible employment practices being one of the most significant. Labour migration and flexible employment practices have seemingly entered into a marriage of convenience: the sectors that have the most flexible employment contracts are also those that employ the most labour migrants. The EU's policy of economic liberalisation seems to be accelerating the transition to flexible employment practices. One possible consequence is that national markets will not only welcome more foreign companies but also more new migrants. The worldwide redistribution of labour also means a large measure of uncertainty as to which occupations will be retained, relocated, or even replaced entirely, for example by IT and other new technologies. Factors of this kind make it exceptionally difficult to predict the future demand for labour, making it a high-risk business to encourage labour migration. After all, no one wants to be saddled with tomorrow's unemployed.

The present publication considers how we can improve how labour migration is managed, a question of undiminished importance despite the current economic crisis and rising unemployment rate. After all, labour migration depends on many other factors. Because other countries also wish to improve their policies, the editors of this book have consulted a number of internationally renowned researchers. The first contribution is by Demetrios Papademetriou, President of the Washington DC-based Migration Policy Institute, who regards the dwindling size of the labour force as one of the key problems of the twenty-first century. In Chapter 2 he argues that migration is one way to solve this problem. Encouraging more migration requires intelligent preparation both by the authorities and by businesses and civil society organisations. One particular issue is how to attract highly skilled workers from outside the EU. The EU Member States will have to do much more than they have done so far to compete with the growing number of countries vying for 'the best and brightest'.

In Chapter 3, George Lemaître of the OECD discusses several ways to identify the needs of the labour market. He argues that scenarios concerning the impact of ageing on the labour market are unsuitable for that purpose. Labour needs are a much more reliable measure in his view, although it is always necessary to take the recruitment and hiring process for foreign employees into account. Using Sweden as an example, he argues that opening up the borders will not lead to an uncontrollable inflow of labour migrants if firm agreements are made between the social partners. To what extent labour migration should be allowed is ultimately a labour market issue, in Lemaître's opinion.

Martin Ruhs and Bridget Anderson share his view. They also note in Chapter 4 that the demand for labour migrants cannot be measured objectively. They argue that employer demand should be viewed with caution. One contingent factor is that the choices employers have are critically influenced by training, education and labour market regulatory policy. In the opinion of Ruhs and Anderson, whether the EU Member States can alleviate labour shortages by attracting more labour migrants, paying higher wages or experimenting with other options is necessarily a political issue that requires a balancing of conflicting interests. The process of balancing those interests should be part of a much wider public debate that also considers which social and economic model we wish to apply in future.

In Chapter 5, Béla Galgóczi and Janine Leschke look at the free movement of workers within the European Union, which increased considerably in scale after the 2004 and 2007 enlargements. European migration patterns were heavily influenced by the transitional measures that were applied, their duration, and by the economic crisis. Both authors are concerned about the huge mismatch between the educational attainment of the EU's Central and Eastern European migrants and the work that they do. They believe that one of the biggest challenges facing European policymakers within the context of the EU's internal labour migration is to resolve this mismatch, which is accompanied by an inefficient distribution of labour between countries.

In Chapter 6, Godfried Engbersen looks at the integration of labour migrants from Central and Eastern Europe in the Netherlands. In his view, there are different patterns of labour migration defined by various forms of transience and settlement. The authorities – local, national and European – should be more concerned about the social repercussions of these patterns for regions and cities. In Engbersen's view, traditional integration policy pays too little attention to the transient nature of the new migration. It also focuses mainly on migrants from outside the EU. In future, it will need to be more closely attuned to the various patterns of migration.

Each of the specialists referred to above makes proposals for improving labour migration in the EU. In Chapter 1, WRR staff members Monique Kremer, Erik Schrijvers and advisory member of the council Jan Willem Holtslag build on these author's most important findings and answer two questions. The first is whether the present form and scale of labour migration will be enough to alleviate the oft-predicted labour shortages. One of the problems they observe is that labour migration policy is largely the result of a series of ad-hoc employer decisions, whereas demographic trends seem to require policy that takes the longer view. The second question is whether labour migration in the EU is sufficiently managed. Their question concerns both the jobs migrants fill in and the wider social context of labour migration.

Kremer, Schrijvers and Holtslag argue that it will take considerable effort to improve the way labour migration is managed. More accurate analyses of future trends are needed to arrive at better policy decisions. If we fail to anticipate future labour market trends, we cannot develop an economically and socially sound labour migration policy. The investment involved in attracting talented workers is also huge because highly skilled migrants can choose between more and more destination countries.

Another point that merits attention is how well newcomers are integrated into the labour market. Because of their uncertain position in the labour market, they have little opportunity to build a solid basis for themselves, although it is clear that some of them are easily employable and will ultimately want to settle in their destination country permanently. In addition, Brussels should take more responsibility for labour mobility, which is one of the crucial policy objectives of the EU. Because the circulation of workers is linked to external social effects, compensation for those effects should be an integral part of European policy.

Given the importance of these issues, the WRR has decided to publish these studies, all of which touch on the future of labour migration in the EU, in a special volume. The WRR expects that they will provide food for thought and inspire public and political debate.

Prof.dr. J.A. Knottnerus
Chairman of the WRR

ACKNOWLEDGEMENTS

The present publication is the result of an internal project group of the WRR consisting of Mr.drs. G. Arts, Dr. W. Asbeek Brusse, Dr. M. Kremer, Drs. G. Nekkers (project coordinator until 1 May 2012), M. Rem MA MBA and Dr. E. Schrijvers (project coordinator from 1 May 2012). D. van Doorn MA and M. Konterman MSc participated briefly as trainees. The project group was chaired by Drs. J.W. Holtslag (advisory member of the WRR).

We would like to thank the many individuals and organisations that helped prepare this publication, to begin with our external authors. The findings reviewed in this publication are based not only on their contributions but also on interviews with a wide variety of persons who shared their knowledge and insights with the grateful members of the project group. We consulted dozens of experts in the private sector, at universities and research institutes, and in government in the Netherlands and elsewhere who are involved in some way or another in migration, integration and labour market issues. Representatives of the Cities of Amsterdam and Rotterdam also kindly agreed to be interviewed by the project group. The interviews produced exceptionally useful knowledge and information.

Our thanks also goes to the participants – the researchers, decision-makers and politicians – who attended three meetings held in the first half of 2012, as did most of the authors of this publication. The meetings covered recent labour market trends, the pattern of migration in Europe, and the relevant policy issues related to labour migration and the integration of labour migrants.

We would also like to express our thanks to High Tech Campus Eindhoven, the Eemshaven and the Rotterdam Port Authorities for their warm reception, guided tours and information. Our international working visits and contacts in the United Kingdom, Australia, Denmark, Sweden, Germany and of course Brussels also led to many new insights. We are grateful to all these organisations and their staff for their assistance.

Within the context of this project, we also asked the independent research agency *Regioplan* to update its 2005 study *Poolshoogte: onderzoek naar juridische constructies en kostenvoordelen bij het inzetten van arbeidskrachten in drie sectoren*. The update was made possible by the WRR in cooperation with the Ministry of the Interior and Kingdom Relations and the Ministry of Social Affairs and Employment. We would like to thank both ministries for supporting this study.

1   HOW TO MAKE MIGRATION WORK

Monique Kremer, Erik Schrijvers and Jan Willem Holtslag

1.1   INTRODUCTION

Labour migration has become inevitable in a Europe without frontiers. In fact, one of the explicit aims of the European Union Member States is to promote the free movement of workers in addition to the free movement of commerce and goods. The underlying idea is that labour shortages in one country can be offset by unemployed workers from other countries. Besides preventing unemployment, an open European labour market also improves economic resilience and allows European regions to specialise, making the European Union more competitive as a whole.

Compared to the United States or Canada, internal mobility in the European Union (EU) is particularly low. Only 2.5 per cent of Europeans live in a EU Member State other than the one in which they were born (Eurostat 2012). The free movement of workers is also quite limited in scale compared to the EU's other 'freedoms'. The objectives set for the EU apparently fail to acknowledge that people base a decision to move elsewhere not only on financial motives but also on language and other cultural and social obstacles (Favell 2008; Bonin et al. 2008).

When the EU welcomed ten new Central and Eastern European Member States in 2004 and 2007, however, internal mobility increased considerably in scale and its complexion also changed. That has had consequences for the Netherlands as well. Although many of the 1.5 million people who left Poland migrated to the United Kingdom, the Netherlands has an estimated 300,000 'new' EU citizens from Central and Eastern Europe (Van der Heijden et al. 2011; Eurostat 2012; Regioplan 2012). The recent crisis has also led to a slight increase in migration from southern Europe (CBS 2012). On top of that, today's migrants have other reasons for choosing the Netherlands. They now come here mainly to work or study. Family migration is much less common (Jennissen 2011a). While family migration from non-EU countries used to dominate, nowadays migration largely means labour migration from other Member States.

Another clear change in the past few decades is the heavy emphasis – at least in policy terms – on recruiting highly skilled workers from outside the Union. As a result, an entirely new type of labour migrant has recently appeared on the scene. Most of the EU Member States, the Netherlands included, have become much more critical when recruiting non-EU citizens. This is referred to as 'managed migration' or '*immigration choisie*'. The migrants who pass the selection process must be highly skilled; such workers are economically useful and unlikely to fall back on social welfare provisions. Low-skilled workers from outside the EU are explicitly kept out. This too has led to a change in the countries of origin. In the Netherlands countries such as India, China and the United States head the league tables when it comes to sending highly skilled workers, although there are still very few of them proportionally speaking.

Economists have pointed out that the current rate of labour migration will not be enough to compensate for such demographic trends as the ageing population and low birth rate. In the long term, the EU will need more labour migrants. That is also the view of the European Commission, which not only wishes to increase internal labour mobility to improve the match between labour market supply and demand, but also foresees a growing need for more migrants from outside the EU – although it has not repeated that opinion since the most recent economic crises broke (see Goldin et al. 2010). It is also the view that a high-value, competitive economy requires highly skilled migrants to be recruited from outside the EU.

The first question addressed in this chapter is whether the present form and scale of labour migration will be sufficient to alleviate the oft-predicted labour shortages. One complicating factor is that the task of recruiting both high-skilled 'knowledge migrants' and EU labour migrants lies largely in the hands of employers, which are keen to fill specific vacancies as quickly as possible. That means that labour migration policy is largely the result of a series of ad hoc employer decisions, whereas demographic trends seem to require policy that takes the longer view. But is it in fact possible to develop a long-term view of labour migration, and what would such a policy entail?

The second question is whether the labour migration in the EU is sufficiently managed? In the past, the EU Member States have not always proved capable of absorbing migrant groups quickly and permanently into their labour markets. The Netherlands is no exception in that regard. For example, the labour market participation rate and skills of former guest workers and their children still lag behind those of the native population (Thomas and Widmaier 2009; Gijsberts et al. 2012). It is therefore no surprise that migration is a highly polarised topic in many European countries, including the Netherlands: half of the population wants to restrict it, while the other half recognises its advantages (Eurobarometer 2012).

Many of the opinions and debates are, however, based on experiences with specific groups of migrants, i.e. guest workers from Morocco and Turkey. The new European migrants are more educated and, unlike the guest workers, can return to their country of origin – something that many of them do (Van Galen et al. 2008; Verschuren et al. 2011). That does not apply for non-EU labour migrants, although they too are more educated – in fact, much more so than most of the new EU labour migrants. The question is whether it makes sense to base future migration policy on the history of guest workers. Ignoring that history altogether is also not an option, however. Even today, many European labour migrants work in insecure jobs. Are we ignoring the integration of today's and tomorrow's labour migrants at our peril? And what role should local, national and EU authorities play in preventing or tackling any problems that may arise?

Later in this chapter, we will explore – drawing in part on the studies by Papademetriou, Lemaître, Ruhs and Anderson, Galgóczi and Leschke, and Engbersen – whether the EU can improve its labour migration policy, both now and in the future. First, however, we will consider how to improve our ability to predict future labour market developments so that we can make better choices in policymaking. One helpful strategy is to take global labour market trends as our point of departure, rather than basing policy solely on quantitative demographic extrapolations (sections 1.2 and 1.3). The next step is to consider how best to recruit workers if they should in fact be needed (1.4). Our conclusion is that the Netherlands must shift the focus from its admissions policy to its knowledge infrastructure and social policy. This would improve its chances of attracting highly skilled employees from within and outside the European Union. The next question is which policy is required once migrants have arrived in the Netherlands. How can we make migration work? That will require a more differentiated integration policy, one that is less concerned with country of origin (EU or non-EU) and more concerned with whether the migrants involved plan to settle in the Netherlands permanently (1.5). Much of the proposed labour migration policy is in the hands of local, regional and national government. The European Union's challenges are addressed in a separate section (1.6). Because the free movement of workers is enshrined at European level, Brussels must also broaden its policy of labour migration; it should not only do more to encourage it, but also to compensate for its negative externalities.

1.2   IMPROVING OUR SCENARIO'S TO EXPLORE THE FUTURE: LINKING LABOUR MIGRATION TO LONG TERM LABOUR MARKET TRENDS

Numerous economists have stated that the ageing population and the low birthrate in the Netherlands will make labour migration unavoidable in future (Theeuwes 2011; Münz 2011; Brakman and Van Witteloostuijn 2010). They see huge labour shortages on the horizon. In 2008, for example, the Labour Participation Committee calculated that by 2040, the Netherlands would have a labour market gap of 700,000 workers. A more recent report calculates that the shortage would amount to approximately 16 per cent of the labour force by 2050 (Berkhout and Van den Berg 2010). The shortage is expected to disappear only after 2060, when the labour force will increase in size slightly.

The above analysis makes for some sombre scenarios. Wages will rise, making the cost of labour in the Netherlands too steep. As a result, jobs will be relocated and businesses will shut down. The welfare state will come under pressure as well, with the 'dependency ratio' – the ratio between the non-working (or dependent) and working (or productive) parts of the population rising from 25 per cent non-working in 2010 to almost 50 per cent in 2050 (Demifer 2011). This means that fewer and fewer people will have to raise more and more money. The ageing of the population will hit particularly hard in the health care sector, the expectation being that a relatively elderly population will require more care and thus more nursing staff. The Netherlands Institute for Social Research (Eggink et al. 2010) estimates that staff shortages in health care will rise to 250,000 by 2030 (see also Colombo et al. 2011). In other words, numerous demographic forecasts confirm that the ageing population and low birth rate will lead to sizeable labour market shortages that require quick, forward-thinking action (Karlsson and Pelling 2011).

But the question is: which forward-thinking action precisely? Demographic forecasts often attempt to make global predictions about the size of the labour shortages that we can expect. They also often link these shortages directly to the need for labour migration. For example, the SEO (2010) believes that labour migration could reduce the Dutch labour shortage from 16 to 13 per cent in 2050. Münz (2011) calculates that labour migration will be necessary no matter which of the various scenarios applies. But such quantitative extrapolations do little to explain what type of labour, with what features and what kind of cross-border labour mobility may be required in future. By definition, they also fall short because they do not take trends in the economy, in productivity and in the related labour market into account.

It is much harder to predict the latter trends than demographic ones, which have a much longer time horizon. Let us not forget that the economic structure is constantly changing. Old industries and occupations disappear, and new ones arise (Goos et al. 2010; Hurley et al. 2011), a process that Schumpeter once referred to as 'creative destruction'. In a subsequent chapter, Lemaître offers us a good illustration. He shows that between 2000 and 2010, the number of young people entering new occupations was three times the number of older people retiring from the workforce. In addition, the outgoing population of retirees from rapidly disappearing occupations far outstripped the incoming population of young workers. As soon as the baby boom generation leaves the labour market, some of their jobs will also disappear. The new generation will not be affected by this creative destruction, since it works in entirely new jobs, few of which existed previously.

Technological innovation and global competitiveness will spur many of the labour market trends of the future. The Netherlands is a good example: new technologies and the relocation of industries abroad have caused much of the routine work, for example in shipbuilding and the automobile industry, to disappear. Administrative and ICT jobs have also been relocated (Witteloostuijn and Hartog 2007; SER 2008). One new, complicating factor in such relocation is what is known as 'task differentiation': it is no longer entire products that are bought and sold, but rather small product components (Akçomak et al. 2010). Technological advances (the Internet) and a high standard of development elsewhere (South Korea, China, India) make it possible to manufacture more and more products all over the world. For example, approximately seventy per cent of the parts that make up the new Boeing 787 Dreamliner are made in more than forty different businesses at more than 130 production sites. The European Centre for the Development of Vocational Training (2010) notes that the economic crises have kicked task differentiation processes into a higher gear.

How these trends will affect the Dutch labour market is open to question. The optimistic scenario is that the Netherlands has precisely the right equipment to link global production processes. In *The Global Auction*, however, Brown et al. (2011) paint a much gloomier picture. In their view, digital Taylorism – dividing up tasks and outsourcing them on the Internet – and the rising tide of Chinese and Indian graduates with much lower wage expectations also mean that much of the high-value work in the West will be relocated. So globalisation will not only affect those in the lower and middle segments of the labour market, but also workers who have long considered themselves safe: Westerners with a good education. On the other hand, the ease of travel and Internet communication may well obviate the need to relocate high-skilled employees for longer periods (Jennissen 2011b). In other words: it is unclear whether high-skilled workers will even be required in future.

Other segments of the labour market face the same uncertainty. One oft-heard prediction is that there will be very few jobs on the lower end of the labour market in future, one reason for the Netherlands and many other EU Member States to close their borders to low-skilled workers from non-EU countries. But as Galgóczi and Leschke demonstrate *in a subsequent chapter*, it is the lower end of the labour market that manifests the most cross-border mobility. There is an ongoing demand for low-skilled labour in such sectors as the meat processing industry, agriculture and horticulture – a demand met largely by labour migrants (Regioplan 2012). The forecasts for the middle segment of the labour market are equally unclear. Globalisation economists (Autor et al. 2003) antici-pate that a large number of occupations in the middle segment will disappear in high-value economies. Conversely, the public's rising expectations and more complex treatment methods may lead to a huge demand for middle-segment workers in the long-term health care sector. That is also true for the technical segment of the labour market, where the introduction of stricter safety stand-ards and more complex machinery has driven the demand for higher skilled workers. ROA (2012) predicts that graduates with a technical or VET health care qualification will have good prospects of finding a job until 2016. It is unclear whether labour migration can meet this particular labour demand, however. It is still uncommon for foreign workers to find jobs in the health care, technical and other sectors (De Lange 2007; Van Dalen et al. 2012).

In summary, it is not at all clear how various segments of the labour market will develop, nor to what extent more workers with which qualifications will be required. We can therefore say very little about how necessary labour migration will actually be.

A second argument favouring a more proactive labour migration policy is often put forward in addition to demographic labour shortages. The idea is that the Netherlands should specialise in high-value labour in order to compete in the global marketplace. Economic models that emphasise the importance of knowl-edge, research and development for economic growth claim that a high level of human capital is needed to promote long-term economic growth and national (or European) competitiveness (Ruhs and Anderson, *present publication*). That is also the idea behind the Europe 2020 strategy, aimed at bolstering the EU's economy (European Commission 2010a). This argument recommends having the largest number of high-skilled workers possible, regardless of the specific demand for labour. One way to achieve this is to recruit talented foreign work-ers, preferably 'the best and the brightest' (Ozgen et al. 2010).

However, as economist Hartog (2011) rightly asserts, simply attracting highly skilled workers will contribute little to the per capita income. Suppose that we only attract the most talented and double the uppermost 5 per cent of our own labour force. That would mean a one-off increase in the per capita income of 7.3 per cent, or half a decade's economic growth. According to Hartog's calcu-lations, we would need to recruit 700,000 foreign workers to achieve this. However, that is only interesting if their knowledge and skills offer added val-ue. In other words, high-skilled foreign workers must have more to offer than the Netherlands' own large and growing population of university graduates. In the UK, the NIESR (George et al. 2012) studied strategically important skills that make a disproportionately large contribution to productivity increases, innovation, and growth in economic sectors in which the UK has a competitive advantage. Many workers from outside the EU were recruited precisely on these grounds. They possessed skills in short supply among domestic workers, for example expertise in specific technological sectors or a good understanding – in both the business and the cultural sense – of operations at international business locations. A Danish study (Malchow-Møller et al. 2011) also showed that productivity in fact rose sharply in companies that had recruited knowledge migrants; because the foreign workers they had recruited gave them a knowledge of foreign markets that they did not previously have, the companies began to export more of their products. The main idea is that a company will gain economic advantages recruiting foreign workers if the latter's knowledge and skills complement rather than compete with those of the existing workforce and if they are also compatible with the country or region's economically strong sectors.

A good labour migration policy therefore requires a knowledge of the relevant country's economy and the way in which its economic structure will change over time. At the moment, labour migration policy – whether it pertains to knowledge migrants from outside the European Union or to the free movement of workers – is determined largely by the *current* situation in the labour market. In other words: the ad-hoc decisions of individual employers provide the basis for 'policymaking', whereas long-term demographic and large-scale global economic trends in fact require a more systematically reasoned approach. Migration policy therefore concentrates on ex post shortages instead of potential demand (Collett and Zuleeg 2008). Developing a more considered, goal-oriented, long-term labour migration policy requires us to have a better picture of the future of the Dutch economy and labour market in a global context.

Abstract shortages (e.g. resulting from the ageing population) are thus not very helpful as a starting point. Following in the footsteps of Collett and Zuleeg (2008), the focus could shift to various skills categories. These authors start by identifying 'scarce skills', a list of shortages that changes over time and requires regular updating, taking into account the changing circumstances in the labour market and the outcomes of previous recruitment campaigns (Lemaître, *present publication*). They then focus on the 'super skilled', the exceptionally talented and productive. Every country wants them, but successful recruitment involves discovering them early and getting them to commit, a strategy that is based on a good understanding of the strengths of one's own economy. Finally, 'soft skills' also play a role and should be part of every labour migrant's skills set. Income, educational and training criteria are by no means good predictors of successful labour market integration, in which cooperation, initiative or a client-friendly attitude are considered increasingly important. It might be possible to explore which skills will become important based on these or other categories.

The Australian government recently made a similar attempt. Drawing on information from stakeholders and various statistics, it developed a number of scenarios for the economy and related labour market profiles so that it could do a better job making labour migration work.

1.3   TOWARDS A SOUNDER RATIONALE IN POLICYMAKING

Having a better idea of where the economy and labour market are headed allows us to base our policy choices on a sounder rationale regarding whether, where, when, and how many labour migrants are needed. What factors do we need to consider?

The first is whether cross-border labour mobility in the EU (which is still limited in scale) will be enough to compensate for any shortages (OECD 2012a). It is often said that the free movement of workers will gradually reduce the wage gap between Western and Eastern Europe. Although the economic and financial crises seem to be widening that gap, in the long run wage convergence could lead to a decline in cross-border labour mobility. It is precisely the huge wage gaps between the Member States that have driven recent labour migration flows. In addition, other Member States are even more concerned than the Netherlands about their ageing populations and declining birth rates. The fertility rate in the Southern and Eastern European Member States is exceptionally low (Papademetriou, *present publication*). Whereas 2.1 children are needed simply to replace their current populations (Demifer 2011), countries such as Spain (1.41) and Poland (1.32) are at the bottom of the fertility rate list. If the entire EU population is shrinking, however, then the question is: what sort of work will European workers do and what sort of work will be done by workers from outside the EU?

The second factor concerns the strategies available to ensure a large enough working population. It is important to realise that supply and demand are not objective facts, making it difficult to predict where labour scarcity and shortages will occur (Ruhs and Anderson, *present publication*). Employers have many different ways of reducing labour market shortages. They can raise wages, improve their employment terms, offer career prospects, relocate jobs elsewhere, replace human labour by technology, train new workers, and – last but not least – recruit labour migrants. In a later chapter, Ruhs and Anderson point out that employers that have access to cheap migrant labour may not consider alternatives. For example, the British health care sector scarcely invests in training anymore. Migrants may therefore unintentionally cause employers to scale back training and career development programmes for workers in the destination country, leading to a deterioration of their employment conditions.

Politics naturally also plays a role by establishing the regulatory frameworks that constrain employers' choices (Ruhs and Anderson, *present publication*). In a Europe without internal borders, labour migration is no longer regulated by applying the traditional migration mechanisms but by the demand (employer) and supply (workers) sides of the labour market. What lies between the two are national and other labour market institutions, for example the minimum wage, collective agreements, employment contracts and social insurance schemes. These sorts of institutions, legislation, rules and agreements have become more important to the regulation of European labour migration than traditional migration mechanisms, which usually focus on admission and border controls. That means that politic should concentrate on a different set of mechanisms, in most cases the labour market.

Sweden offers a good example. After the EU's enlargement in 2004, it welcomed far fewer labour migrants from Central and Eastern Europe than the United Kingdom, although neither country – unlike most of the other EU Member States – introduced transitional measures (Galgóczi and Lescke, *present publication*). However, the UK's minimal regulatory framework for wages and employment conditions made it advantageous for employers to recruit large numbers of EU workers. That cost advantage was largely absent in the Swedish labour market, most of which is covered by various collective agreements. Comparing the two countries clearly shows that in a Europe with open borders, institutional characteristics of national labour markets play a crucial role in determining the nature and scale of labour migration (Lemaître, *present publication*).

But politics can also influence employers' options in many other ways. Besides influencing the shape of the labour market itself, policymakers can emphasise certain scarce disciplines or skills in the education system, raise the retirement age, increase the labour force participation rates among less active groups (including migrants who already live in the Netherlands), promote a more dynamic labour market, encourage training on the job, and so on (Papademetriou, *present publication*).

These strategies entail complex trade-offs, however, as each one involves a wide range of economic and social costs and benefits, both in the shorter and – in particular – the longer term. Tackling the labour shortages in the health care sector, for example, will require a major financial investment in education, something that France has already undertaken (OECD 2010). In the Netherlands, it is often claimed that labour shortages in the health care system can be resolved by having all part-time employees work full time from now on. But that also comes at a 'price', for example more employees calling in sick due to the strain of their jobs, or an extra investment in child care. On top of this, alternatives are not always readily available, or government is not capable of putting them into place. When it comes to rapidly changing disciplines with an international focus (for example in IT or the creative industry), no single educational programme is capable of providing the relevant knowledge and skills at short notice – if indeed formal schooling is even the most suitable context (Kolb et al. 2004; Salt 2008).

Any long-term labour mobility policy will therefore have to consider the economic and social trade-offs of the various strategies for meeting the demand for labour. Deploying Central and Eastern European workers in low-paying sectors such as manufacturing, meat processing and horticulture (Regioplan 2012) is one example of a difficult trade-off: is the added value of such sectors to the Dutch economy more important than the risk that they will only survive by employing migrants on a massive scale, with all the associated social and economic implications for both the migrants and society as a whole? Or are certain industries simply so important that migrant labour is unavoidable? If that is the case in the horticulture sector, for example, then why not forego the annual ritual negotiations between the Minister of Social Affairs and Employment and employers about recruiting seasonal workers from abroad?

Or, as Ruhs and Anderson correctly conclude in a later chapter of this book:

> "the question about alternative responses to shortages is an inherently normative issue that does not have a single 'right' answer. Deciding whether the optimal response to shortages should be additional migrants, higher wages, or some other option is a necessarily political issue that requires a balancing of competing interests."

In their view, such interests must be balanced within the context of a broader public debate, one that focuses on the social and economic model that we want for the Netherlands and Europe, and how migration fits into that system.

1.4 BEYOND ADMISSION POLICY: RECRUITING THE HIGHER-SKILLED

Suppose that the Netherlands needs foreign workers who have specific knowledge and skills. Will they actually come? There is little doubt concerning low-skilled workers: they will always be eager to migrate to Europe and the Netherlands, according to Papademetriou and Lemaître in later chapters of this book. The more important question is whether the high-skilled workers will – and by that we mean the scarce and super skilled professionals. The Dutch Government's 2004 Knowledge Migrants Scheme has increased the number of high-skilled foreign workers from outside the EU. In 2010, for example, 5,561

IT professionals, most of them Indian, entered the Netherlands (Vleugel 2011). Against all expectations, however, the influx has remained relatively small, certainly when compared to such countries as Sweden. Only 2.4 per cent of the Netherlands' total labour force is a scarce or super skilled migrant worker (Chaloff and Lemaître 2009; Boston Consulting Group 2012). According to Papademetriou (*present publication*), the issue is no longer how Western countries will choose highly skilled migrants, but how they – the highly skilled – will choose us. How do we tempt the best and the brightest to come to the Netherlands?

Papademetriou argues that many non-EU countries – in particular the fast-growing economies – will soon be seeking to recruit talented foreigners as well. The EU Member States will not just be competing with China, India, Brazil or the United States. Turkey, Indonesia, Mexico and South Africa are also rapidly developing into major competitors for international labour migration. The 'battle for brains' is therefore set to become even fiercer in future.

Many European countries have therefore developed policies supporting the recruitment of high-skilled labour migrants from outside the EU (Zincone et al. 2011; Chaloff and Lemaître 2009). That is also true of the Netherlands, which has one of the most straightforward systems in the world for admitting high-skilled workers: migrants need only comply with an income requirement to be able to accept a job offer from a Dutch employer (INDIAC 2007; Van Oers and Minderhoud 2012). In 2009, the EU introduced the Blue Card, meant to regulate the recruitment of high-skilled migrants from non-EU Member States. Companies can apply for a Blue Card (analogous to the USA's Green Card) if they wish to recruit knowledge workers from outside the EU. Because many countries were unwilling to transfer this authority to Brussels (United Kingdom) or have more lenient admission rules (Netherlands), the Blue Card is generally regarded as a failure (Cerna 2010).

But a simplified, fast-track admissions procedure is not enough to recruit knowledge migrants. Papademetriou (*present publication*) identifies three sets of variables that can be used to encourage highly skilled migrants to migrate to the European Union. In addition to a robust and invigorating knowledge infrastructure, he believes that the presence of other talented professionals is very important. After all, talented people want to work with other talented people. The second set of variables consists of more general conditions, for example a fair and generous social system (including the possibility of transferring accrued pension rights), an attractive lifestyle and environment, and a tolerant and safe society. The third set of variables – the immigration regime – plays only a limited role in his view, an opinion also held by Lemaître, who claims in his chapter that there is no added value to a point system: it does not make countries more or less attractive to migrants. At most, a point system makes the admission requirements clearer.

Countries such as the Netherlands and Denmark have therefore introduced other measures to attract knowledge migrants, for example various tax incentives. Studies show, however, that knowledge migrants also base their choice of destination country on factors other than financial ones. They consider such important matters as a dense infrastructure of enterprises, universities and research institutions and an attractive lifestyle and environment (Berkhout et al. 2010).

If the Netherlands wants to implement a long-term strategy of attracting complementary skills, it must invest in an open society, social welfare provisions and a well-organised national and (in some cases) regional knowledge infrastructure. The latter is important not only for attracting talented foreign workers, but also for ensuring that knowledge migrants provide added value. Labour mobility policy therefore involves much more than the national admissions policy, which is always the focal point of attention; it also means investing in the knowledge infrastructure, in innovation, and in social policy. The latter factor is one in which the European Union also plays a major role, since cross-border coordination of social welfare entitlements and provisions have largely become an EU matter. We will return to this topic later.

1.5   TOWARDS A MORE DIFFERENTIATED INTEGRATION POLICY AND BETTER JOBS

Even if the Netherlands invests in training, raises the retirement age and has everyone working full time, inward and outward labour migration will continue. Although the present generation of labour migrants is very different from the guest workers of the 1960s and 1970s, the integration and emancipation of newcomers continues to be a major concern. On top of everything else, the labour market has changed dramatically: the Netherlands now has an exceptionally large percentage of flexible workers by European standards. A lot of migrants have flexible employment contracts that offer little security.

The Dutch labour market, educational system and welfare state have not always been capable of helping previous generations of migrants – and their children – acquire more skills and find better jobs (Crul 2012; WRR 2006 and 2007). Lemaître cites OECD studies showing that Europe, including the Netherlands, has been much less successful than traditional immigrant societies (e.g. Australia and Canada) at addressing social and educational disadvantage among the children of low-skilled migrants. Their PISA scores lag far behind the scores of non-migrants' children, for example (cf. Gijsberts et al. 2012). Problems related to the integration and educational attainment of earlier migrants and their children colour the current debate about labour migration to a considerable extent.

However, analyses of such disadvantages are based on a specific and unique generation of labour migrants, i.e. the guest workers. Today's labour migration is considerably more heterogeneous. Galgóczi and Leschke (*present publication*) emphasise the multifaceted nature of labour migration in the European Union. They show that the free movement of workers encompasses differing, co-existing forms of labour mobility. There are self-employed persons who work abroad, and posted workers employed in the international service sector. There is also internal mobility in multinational enterprises, with workers transferring to work locations abroad without changing employers. Some of these 'mobile employees' spend only a short period of time working in another country.

Engbersen (*present publication*) shows that the recent labour migration flows from Central and Eastern Europe fall into four patterns. Labour migrants who conform to the pattern of *temporary, circular migration* do not mix much with the Dutch and are mainly interested in earning money that they can invest in their country of origin. The pattern of *transnational or binational migration* concerns migrants who have put down roots in the Netherlands but maintain close ties with their own country. *Settlement migration* is prevalent among persons who have had children in the Netherlands and whose partner does not live (or no longer lives) in their country of origin. The pattern of *footloose migration* applies when the migrants are only in the Netherlands a relatively short time but also have little contact with their country or origin. Many migrants in this category have a low level of education.

Dutch integration policy bears little relation to these differentiated forms of labour migration. It is remarkably that policy focuses mainly on the integration of non-EU citizens, who are required to assimilate, learn Dutch, and so on. Because of their educational background and high incomes, knowledge migrants are exempt from these requirements. EU citizens are also not required to comply with any integration obligations. Such requirements would be unlawful anyway, because EU citizens must be treated as equals; the authorities are not allowed to discriminate between Dutch citizens and EU citizens. At the same time, it is clear that many EU workers and knowledge migrants could use and in fact often want assistance. That is true whether they come to the Netherlands temporarily or live here for a longer period of time and wish to settle here with their families.

It therefore makes more sense not to take country of origin (EU or non-EU) as the starting point for integration policy, but rather the degree to which newcomers actually intend to settle in the Netherlands. Unlike Turkish and Moroccan guest workers, but similar to their Spanish and Italian counterparts, some of the new EU labour migrants do in fact return to their country of origin. Many EU citizens, especially the skilled professionals and some of the low-skilled Poles, only remain in the Netherlands for a brief period of time, often less than a year (Nicolaas 2011). Many knowledge migrants, most of whom come from India and work in the it sector, also stay only a couple of years. A certain proportion of EU citizens and knowledge migrants do wish to settle in the Netherlands, however. Settlement migration is particularly common among migrants who have been in the Netherlands several years, have started a family, and have children enrolled in a Dutch school.

The Netherlands needs to develop a mechanism for dealing with these various labour migration patterns (Engbersen, *present publication*). At the moment, the focus tends to be on adequate housing for newcomers, especially those who are here temporarily. But a long-term housing policy is also important in preventing concentrations of labour migrants in disadvantaged neighbour-hoods, a pattern seen in the past. To support the assimilation of labour migrants who intend to remain in the Netherlands for a longer period of time, they should have access to publicly financed language courses – something that the European Union can also assist with (as we will discuss below). In addition, the Netherlands should invest more in teaching the children of EU migrants that wish to settle here. Despite all this, we cannot expect much of transients; integration must be voluntary in their case. They should, however, have access to language courses, regardless of their nationality, because the dividing line between temporary and permanent residence is a fluid one. But those who do settle here can and should be expected to do more, even if they are EU citizens. They, in turn, should be able to expect more from Dutch society, the authorities and employers. The main issue, however, is that Dutch integration policy should be more differentiated, in line with the life course of the migrants themselves. Whether labour migrants come from within or outside the EU is irrelevant. What counts is where they plan to settle.

The labour market also influences the integration and emancipation of labour migrants. Many Central and Eastern European workers are flexible labour migrants: they work in the Netherlands on temporary contracts, and are often deployed through specialist employment agencies (Berkhout et al. 2010). That was also shown in a recent study by Regioplan (2012), carried out on behalf of the Scientific Council for Government Policy (WRR). According to Regioplan, the preference for flexible contracts is related in part to the temporary nature of the work involved, such as seasonal work. But flexible contracts also offer the biggest cost advantages. This goes specifically for self-employed workers, who more or less set their own rates. Increasingly, employers use migrant workers deployed through employment agencies to gain huge cost advantages, either by legitimate or illegitimate means; they may hire in temporary workers employed on foreign employment contracts who are thus required to pay tax and social insurance premiums in another country, or remunerate workers in kind (housing and medical insurance) so that they can then pay them lower wages. Another striking phenomenon is that the wages paid to Central and Eastern European migrants working through employment agencies do not appear to have kept pace with inflation.

These sorts of practices are not, by definition, criminal, and they even offer labour migrants certain benefits, since their wages are still considerably higher than those paid in their country of origin. Their home countries also benefit, since the migrants tend to spend their earnings after their return or send part of their wages home during their stay abroad. The fact that some groups of foreign workers are prepared to work for lower wages and under poorer working conditions makes them vulnerable to exploitation, however (Ruhs and Anderson, *present publication*). According to estimates, an alarmingly large number of labour migrants (more than 100,000) are deployed in the Netherlands through fraudulent recruitment agencies (Walz et al. 2010). A robust labour market policy such as Sweden's, which focuses on enforcing collective agreements, minimum wages and working conditions, offers a good defence against such shady practices (Lemaître, *present publication*). A higher level of enforcement, aided by the unions and employers' associations, may well hamper cross-border labour mobility but it will also help to regulate migrant labour. One question is whether 10,000+ small employment agencies can be properly regulated and monitored under current legislation.

Working in an endless series of low-paying, temporary jobs does not give labour migrants who wish to settle in the Netherlands a good basis for social and economic integration and empowerment. Galgóczi and Leschke (*present publication*) show that many EU labour migrants work far below their skills level. Given the huge wage gap between the sending and receiving countries, that is not really an issue in the short term. But the situation is otherwise for those who stay in the receiving country. They need better jobs, jobs suited to their ability, jobs that offer more security so that they can contribute (more) to society. That means that it is crucial to invest in labour migrants who wish to settle in the Netherlands, with both the migrants themselves and the local, national and European authorities investing in education, language training, and job opportunities. The danger now is that no one – neither the employers nor the employment agencies – feels responsible for them.

Because most of the EU migrants go abroad mainly for work, it is the employers that should ensure their wellbeing, especially when the employers themselves have recruited the workers (Papademetriou, *present publication*). Migration is an issue of distribution, claims Hartog (2011): the costs and benefits of migration are distributes to different parties. In the past, the benefits accrued mainly to employers. In 2001, the WRR calculated that migration represented a 3 per cent decline in GNP for workers and a 3.14 per cent increase in GNP for investors. The UK's Migration Advisory Committee (2012) recently made a similar calculation. It is unlikely that anything has changed in the Netherlands since then. In fact, the introduction of flexible employment practices at the lower end of the Dutch labour market has been a facilitator and catalyst for European labour mobility. Many employers have recruited relatively inexpensive workers this way (Ruhs and Anderson, *present publication*). Nevertheless, employers scarcely play any role at all in the integration of EU workers (Collett 2012). Some of the cost advantages that they gain by recruiting migrants could be used to help the workers acquire work-related knowledge and skills, including proficiency in Dutch (Engbersen, *present publication*).

1.6   EUROPEAN POLICY: STIMULATE AND COMPENSATE

So far the EU has worked hard to remove barriers to the mobility of EU citizens, based on the idea that people should be able to study and work in the Member States that offer them the most advantages. But some barriers remain (European Commission 2010b). Besides facilitating and stimulating cross-border labour mobility, the EU could also do more to compensate for the negative social effects resulting from the circulation of workers.

In *Moving beyond demographics*, a foresight study concerning the future of labour migration in Europe, the Swedish think tank Global Utmaning (Karlsson and Pelling 2011) asserts that the EU's migration policy has reached an impasse. The Member States' joint 1999 statement, setting out their aim of a coherent and comprehensive European migration policy seems farther away than ever, in part owing to the economic crisis. The sharp rise in unemployment has also put the demand for foreign workers on hold in many countries. With huge uncertainty regarding the future demand for labour, it would nevertheless be advisable to introduce a number of precautionary measures.

One would be to continue harmonising social insurance entitlements, because the discrepancies are a major impediment to mobility among high-skilled workers. Some entitlements are portable within the EU. Harmonisation helps workers avoid double payment of social insurance contributions, or prevents their losing coverage because they fall between two stools – i.e. between the legislation that applies in two different Member States. The problematic port-ability of supplementary pensions continues to be a huge obstacle to labour mobility in the EU, however, especially for older or higher skilled workers (Bonin et al. 2008; OECD 2012b: 70). At the moment, most of the mobility is at the lower end of the labour market. By making pension entitlements more 'mobile' as well, workers in the middle and higher segments of the EU labour market will be more inclined to move to one of the other Member States when suitable work is available.

Another important issue is how to deal with long-term unemployment. During the economic crisis, migrant labour from Central and Eastern Europe served mainly as a buffer. This led in 2010 to the Netherlands having a larger percentage of unemployed EU workers than unemployed Dutch citizens (Galgózci and Leschke, *present publication*). The question is: who is respon-sible for unemployed migrant workers? Some Member States, including the Netherlands, want to make it harder for EU workers to access their national as-sistance schemes, for example by making benefits contingent on a longer period of residence. That is entirely logical and understandable as a national policy rationale because it prevents labour migrants from claiming social welfare entitlements to which they have made only a minimal contribution. From the EU perspective, however, it does not offer a long-term strategy for dealing with unemployment and loss of income. Apart from that, such measures are likely to reduce labour mobility.

The problem can be tackled more creatively. As Engbersen (*present publication*) indicates, the EU Member States will need to explore how best to promote remigration options among EU workers who are no longer able to support themselves. After all, EU citizens cannot simply be sent back to their country of origin. In addition, more effort can be made to harmonise national assistance benefits at EU level, with benefits being set off between Member States much in the way that insurance is. Another option is to establish an EU social safety net that would go into effect as soon as EU labour migrants are unable to access the social welfare schemes of the country in which they are employed.

If the Member States respond to the economic crisis by cutting the length of time benefits recipients collect unemployment, such options will become a matter of urgency, since EU citizens will need to claim national assistance bene-fits sooner than they have been. If access to national assistance is also restricted, there is a danger that existing social problems – petty crime, homelessness, anti-social behaviour – will increase sharply. That is why the EU will have to develop an EU-wide social policy that deals more effectively with unemploy-ment.

In addition, the EU may be able to assist the Member States in supporting the integration of EU workers. This would mean setting aside a larger budget within the existing European financial institutions (Collett 2012). The European Integration Fund, for example, funds integration programmes in the Member States, but these programmes are officially limited to the integration of migrants from outside the EU. The European Social Fund, meant to support the social inclusion of vulnerable groups, is sometimes used to fund services supporting the integration of mobile EU workers. Such practices should be given a more permanent basis in policy, since EU workers sometimes also need help integrating in their destination country. It would be a major step forward if both EU and non-EU workers could make official use of integration programmes funded by the EU.

Another issue that calls for EU involvement is the problems that migration causes for the wider surroundings. According to IZA (2008), the positive economic effects of European labour mobility appear to outweigh the negative effects, generally speaking. For example, 60 per cent of the EU's remittances consist of funds circulating within the EU. The money that Romanian, Slovakian and Bulgarian migrants send back home surpasses the aid their countries receive from Brussels – a fact that, until recently, was also true of Portugal (Moré 2011).

But tension does arise locally. In a later chapter, Engbersen notes that the new labour migration gives rise to specific social problems that are tangible mainly at local and regional level. In the Netherlands, it is in regions such as Westland and Brabant that the consequences are becoming apparent. Sumption and Somerville (2010) have observed that local authorities in the UK also have trouble coping when large numbers of 'new Europeans' suddenly appear on the scene. In other words, it is a problem that many other EU Member States are also facing. The EU could support the countless local programmes and initiatives that have been developed in the meantime to deal with this problem.

Finally, the EU needs to change its attitude towards the world beyond its borders. One of the few areas in which the EU's migration policy has made progress in recent years is in guarding its external borders. Papademetriou (*present publication*) argues that controlling illegal migration successfully will indeed be one of the biggest challenges of the coming decades. In his view, if the EU is to think strategically about the future of labour migration in Europe though, it must start viewing the countries outside its borders more as partners and economic resources, for example by investing in building their human capital stocks. If it ever does become necessary to recruit foreign workers, the Middle East and North Africa will be obvious sources of human capital owing to their youthful populations. By building on existing partnerships, including in labour migration and training, Europe can kill two birds with one stone, says Papademetriou. It can offer workers and their families opportunities for growth, create a growing class of consumers, and enable future migrants to do better for themselves in Europe and offer greater value to the society in which they live. In Papademetriou's view, this is the only way to rewrite the 'sorry narrative' about guest worker migration in the 1960s and 1970s.

1.7   MAKING MIGRATION WORK

Labour migration policy should be much more closely aligned with the future of the Dutch labour market in a global economy. The starting point for policymaking should not be quantitative extrapolations of the ageing population and low fertility rates, but a much more comprehensive analysis of how the demand for labour will develop in future. Demographic trends would be only one of the many variables in this analysis. A study of this kind could lead to some surprising conclusions. Perhaps the Netherlands will actually need more foreign workers in the middle segment of the labour market, and fewer at the top end. The labour demand at the lower end may also turn out to be long term and consistent in nature.

Such analyses can provide the basis for tackling three important policy issues. Recruiting foreign workers is only one of the mechanisms for ensuring a properly functioning labour market. First of all, any long-term strategy for cross-border labour mobility will have to consider the economic and social trade-offs of the various strategies for meeting the labour demand. Second, such analyses should help clarify the extent to which labour mobility in the European Union can 'solve' the labour market demand and what categories of non-EU workers should be recruited. It is important for the EU to recruit workers from nearby regions, such as the Middle East and North Africa, but that will require long preparation and a long-term investment, for example in existing trade relations and development partnerships. Third, much of the present focus is on attracting high-skilled workers. Having a clearer view of the future makes it possible to identify precisely which complementary skilled professionals will be required. After all, economic growth depends on more than simply recruiting highly skilled workers. More effort should in any event be made to develop a more comprehensive policy on the recruitment of skilled professionals from abroad. A lenient admission policy is not the key to attracting talented professionals. It is more important to invest in the knowledge infrastructure and in social policy.

Labour migration within the EU now tends to be concentrated at the lower end of the labour market. That makes the integration and emancipation of foreign workers an important issue, even if these workers retain their nationalities as EU citizens. The differentiated forms of labour mobility require policymakers to focus more on whether newcomers intend to settle in their destination country, rather than taking EU citizenship as the starting point. Many labour migrants will only stay in the Netherlands temporarily and therefore need access to a flexible system of social welfare entitlements. But a considerable number will also remain in the Netherlands, and it is important that they integrate properly into Dutch society. To avoid repeating the history of the guest workers, government and employers must invest in this group of migrants – something that the migrants themselves can also be expected to do. If the Netherlands aspires to make migration work, it must also offer this group better jobs. At the moment, too many of the new Europeans still work below their ability, through employment agencies. Because employers have the most to gain financially from this system, they can also do more to give foreign workers better opportunities in the labour market.

Finally, the EU's wish to improve the level of cross-border labour mobility requires it to focus on its agreed objectives, for example the portability of social insurance entitlements (especially supplementary pensions). It should also look more closely at the social repercussions of increased labour mobility for cities and regions. To promote mobility and ensure a fair distribution of the burden between countries and regions, the EU must make firmer agreements concerning a European social safety net and about using European funding to welcome, accommodate, and integrate EU labour migrants. Circulation and compensation should go hand in hand.

REFERENCES

Akçomak, S. I., L. Borghans and B. ter Weel (2010) 'Measuring and Interpreting Trends in the Division of Labour in the Netherlands', CPB Discussion Paper 161, November 2010.

Autor, D.H., F. Levy and R.J. Murnane (2003) 'The Skill Content of recent Technological Change: an Empirical Explanation', *The Quarterly Journal of Economics* 118, 4: 1279-1334.

Berkhout, E. and E. van den Berg (2010) *Bridging the Gap: International Database on Employment and Adaptable Labour*, Amsterdam: SEO.

Berkhout, E., T. Smit and M. Volkerink (2010) *Wat beweegt kennismigranten?*, SEO Economisch Onderzoek.

Bonin, H., W. Eichhorst, C. Florman, M.O. Hansen, L. Skiöld, J. Stuhler, K. Tatsiramos, H. Thomasen and K.F. Zimmermann (2008) *Geographic Mobility in the European Union: Optimising its Economic and Social Benefits*, IZA Research Report 19.

Boston Consultancy Group (2012) NL 2030. *Contouren van een nieuw Nederlands verdienmodel*, October 2012.

Brakman, S. and A. van Witteloostuijn (2010) 'Wie gevolgen vergrijzing wil opvangen moet niet xenofoob zijn', *Me Judice* 29 December 2010.

Brown, Ph., H. Lauder and D. Ashton (2011) *The Global Auction. The Broken Promises of Education, Jobs and Incomes*, Oxford: Oxford University Press.

CEDEFOP (2010) *Skills Supply and Demand in Europe; Medium-Term Forecast up to 2020*, Luxemburg.

Centraal Bureau voor de Statistiek (2012) *Toename immigratie door EU-burgers*, CBS press release pb. 12-011.

Cerna, L. (2010) 'The EU Blue Card: a Bridge too far?', Paper prepared for the Fifth Pan-European Conference on EU Politics, Portugal, 23-26 June 2010.

Chaloff, J. and G. Lemaître (2009) 'Managing Highly-Skilled Labour Migration: a Comparative Analysis of Migration Policies and Challenges in OECD-Countries', OECD *Social and Employment and Migration Working Papers* 79.

Collett, E. (2012) 'The Integration Needs of Mobile EU Citizens: Impediments and Opportunities', *Paper for the Dutch-German Conference on Free Movement and Participation of EU-Citizens*, 3-4 September 2012, Rotterdam.

Collett, E. and F. Zuleeg (2008) 'Soft, Scarce and Super Skills: Sourcing the Next Generation of Migrant Workers in Europe', Migration Policy Institute (www.migrationpolicy. org/transatlantic/scarceskills.pdf).

Colombo, F. et al. (2011) *Help Wanted? Providing and Paying for Long-Term Care*, OECD Publishing www.oecd.org/health/longtermcare/helpwanted.

Commissie Arbeidsparticipatie (2008) *Naar een toekomst die werkt. Advies Commissie Arbeidsparticipatie*, June 16, Den Haag.

Crul, M., J. Schneider and F. Lelie (2012) *The European Second Generation Compared. Does the Integration Context Matter?*, Amsterdam: Amsterdam University Press.

Dalen, H. van, K. Henkes, W. Conen and J. Schippers (2012) *Dilemma's rond langer doorwerken. Europese werkgevers aan het woord*, NIDI.35.

Demifer (2011) Final Report, (www.espon.eu/export/sites/default/Documents/ Projects/AppliedResearch/1FinalReport/Final report demifer incl ISBN Feb 2011. PDF).

Eggink, E., D. Oudijk and I. Woittiez (2010) *Zorgen voor zorg. Ramingen van de vraag naar personeel in verplaging en verzorging tot 2030*, Den Haag: Sociaal en Cultureel Planbureau.

Eurobarometer (2012) *Awareness of Home Affairs*, Special Eurobarometer 380, (http:// ec.europa.eu/public_opinion/archives/ebs/ebs_380_en.pdf).

European Commission (2010a) *Europe 2020. A European Strategy for Smart, Sustainable and Inclusive Growth*, COM (2010) 2020 final.

European Commission (2010b) *EU Citizenship Report 2010: Dismantling the Obstacles to EU Citizens' Rights*, COM 603, Brussels.

Eurostat (2012) *Population and Social Conditions* 31/2012.

Favell, A. (2008) *Eurocities and Eurostars. Free Movement and Mobility in a Integrating Europe*, Malden: Blackwell.

Gaalen, R. van, J. Ooijevaar and G. Bijwaard (2008) Eerder verblijf in Nederland vergroot kans op vertrek én terugkomst, p. 39-43 in *Bevolkingstrends: statistisch kwartaalblad over de demografie van Nederland*, first quarter: Centraal Bureau voor de Statistiek.

George, A., M. Lalani, G. Mason, H. Rolfe and C. Bondibeni (2012) *Skilled Immigration and Strategically Important Skills in the UK Economy*, NIESR.

Gijsberts, M, W. Huijnk and J. Dagevos (2012) *Jaarrapport integratie 2011*, Sociaal en Cultureel Planbureau, Den Haag.

Goldin, I., G. Cameron and M. Balarajan (2010) *Exceptional People. How Migration Shaped Our World and Will Define Our Future*, Princeton and Oxford: Princeton University Press.

Goos, M., A. Manning and A. Salomons (2010) 'Explaining Job Polarization in Europe: the Role of technology, Globalization and Institutions', *CEP Discussion Paper* 1026, November 2010.

Hartog, J. (2011) 'Is de maat nou echt vol?', TPEdigitaal 5, 4: 1-16.

Heijden, P.G.M. van der, M. Cruyff and G. van Gils (2011) *Aantallen geregistreerde en niet-geregistreerde burgers uit MOE-landen die in Nederland verblijven. Rapportage schattingen 2008 en 2009*, Utrecht.

Heyma, A., E. Berkhout and S. van der Werff (2011) *De economische impact van arbeidsmigratie: verdringingseffecten 1999-2008*, Amsterdam: SEO.

Hurley, J., D. Storrie and J. Jungblut (2011) 'Shifts in the Job Structure in Europe During the Great Crisis', *European Foundation for the Improvement of Living and Working Conditions*, Luxemburg.

INDIAC (2007) *Hoog opgeleide migranten uit derde landen. Voorwaarden voor toegang en verblijf in Nederland*, Den Haag.

IZA (2008) 'Geographic Mobility in the European Union: Optimising its Social and Economic Benefits, IZA Research Reports 19.

Jennissen, R.P.W. (ed.) (2011a) *De Nederlandse migratiekaart. Achtergronden en ontwikkelingen van verschillende migratietypen*, Den Haag (www.wodc.nl/onderzoeksdatabase/migratiekaart.aspx).

Jennissen, R.P.W. (2011b) 'Arbeidsmigratie en de daarmee gepaard gaande gezinsmigratie naar Nederland', TPEdigitaal 5, 4: 17-36.

Karlsson, J.O. and L.Pelling (eds.) *Moving beyond Demographics. Perspectives for a Common European Migration Policy*, Stockholm.

Kolb, H., S. Murteira, J. Peixoto and C. Sabino (2004) 'Recruitment and Migration in the ICT Sector, p. 147-178 in M. Bommes, K. Hoesch, U. Hunger and H. Kolb (eds.) *Organisational Recruitment and Patterns of Migration. Interdependencies in an Integrating Europe*, Imis-beiträge 25: Universität Osnabrück.

Lange, T. de (2007) *Staat, markt en migrant: de regulering van arbeidsmigratie naar Nederland 1945-2006*, Den Haag: Boom.

Malchow-Møller, N., J.R. Munch and J. R. Skasen (2011) 'Do Foreign Experts Increase Productivity of Domestic Firms?, IZA *Discussion Paper* 6001, October 2011.

Migration Advisory Committee (2012) *Analysis of the Impacts of Migration*, London.

Moré, I. (2011) 'The Case for a European Union Policy on Remittances', p 110-118 in J.O. Karlsson and L. Pelling (eds.) *Moving Beyond Demographics. Perspectives for a Common European Migration Policy*, Stockholm.

Münz, R. (2011) 'The Future of Europe's Labour Force – With and without International Migration', p.15-26 in J.O. Karlsson and L. Pelling (eds.) *Moving beyond Demographics. Perspectives for a Common European Migration Policy*, Stockholm.

Nicolaas, N (2011) 'Ruim helft Poolse immigranten vertrekt weer', p.32-36 in *Bevolkingstrends* 59, first quarter.

OECD (2012a) *Free Movement of Workers and Labour Market Adjustment. Recent Experiences from OECD-Countries and the European Union*, OECD Publishing.

OECD (2012b) *Economic Surveys: European Union.*

OECD (2010) *International Migration of Health Workers. Improving International Coroperation to Adress the Global Health Workforce Crisis*, (www.oecd.org/migration/mig/44783473.pdf).

Oers, R. van, and P.E. Minderhoud (2012) 'The Dutch Position in the 'Battle for Brains', an Overview of Dutch Policy and Legislation on Highly Skilled Labour Migration', *Nijmegen Migration Law Working Papers* Series 2012/01.

Ozgen, C., P. Nijkamp and J. Poot (2010) 'Immigration and Innovation in European Regions, Draft 15 July (www.business.otago.ac.nz/econ/seminars/Abstracts/Poot.pdf).

ROA (2011) *De arbeidsmarkt naar opleiding en beroep tot 2016*, Researchcentrum voor Onderwijs en Arbeidsmarkt: Maastricht.

Regioplan (2012) '*Update Poolshoogte. Onderzoek naar juridische constructies en*

kostenvoordelen bij het inzetten van Poolse arbeidskrachten in drie sectoren',
Amsterdam.

Salt, J. (2008) 'Managing New Migrations in Europe: Concept and Reality in the ICT
Sector', p. 37 in C. Bonifazi, M. Okólski, J. Schoorl, P. Simon (eds.) *International
Migration in Europe. New Trends and New Methods of Analysis*, Amsterdam:
Amsterdam University Press.

Sociaal-Economische Raad (2008) *Advies duurzame globalisering: een wereld te winnen*,
Den Haag.

Sumption, M. and W. Somerville (2010) *The UK's New Europeans. Progress and Challenges five Years after Accession*, Equality and Rights Commission.

Theeuwes, J. (2011) 'Gaten vullen met immigranten?', p. 151-169 in Wim Drees Stichting
(eds.) *Jaarboek overheidsfinanciën 2011*, Den Haag: Sdu.

Thomas, L. and S. Widmaier (2009) 'Children of Immigrants in the Labour Markets
of EU and OECD Countries: An Overview', OECD *Social, Employment and
Migration Working Papers 97*.

Verschuren, S., R. van Gaalen and H. Nicolaas (2011) 'Arbeidsmigratie, volgmigratie en
retourmigratie in de periode 2000–2006', *Bevolkingstrends*, second quarter:
68-78.

Vleugel, M.J. (2011) *Reguliere migratietrends 2008-2010. De reguliere migratie van onder-
danen van derde landen naar Nederland en de EU in beeld*, Rijswijk: Immigratie-
en Naturalisatiedienst.

Walz, C.P., B. Frouws and D.H. Grijpstra (2010) *Grenzen stellen. Omvang van en maatregelen tegen malafide praktijken in de uitzendbranche*, Zoetermeer.

Wetenschappelijke Raad voor het Regeringsbeleid (2001) *Nederland als immigratiesa-
menleving*, Den Haag: Sdu.

Wetenschappelijke Raad voor het Regeringsbeleid (2006) *De verzorgingsstaat herwogen*, Amsterdam: Amsterdam University Press.

Wetenschappelijke Raad voor het Regeringsbeleid (2007) *Identificatie met Nederland*,
Amsterdam: Amsterdam University Press.

Witteloostuijn, A. van and J. Hartog (2007) 'Mondialisering van de arbeidsmarkt', ESB
4514S: 36-40.

Zincone, G., R. Penninx and M. Borkert (eds.) (2011) *Migration Policy Making in
Europe. The Dynamics of Actors and Contexts in Past and Present*, Amsterdam:
Amsterdam University Press.

2 THE GLOBAL AND EUROPEAN NEIGHBOURHOOD MIGRATION SYSTEMS: TRENDS, POLICY CHOICES, GOVERNANCE CHALLENGES AND A LOOK AHEAD

Demetrios G. Papademetriou

2.1 INTRODUCTION

International migration, a key by-product of globalisation, is already one of this century's unavoidable issues. It is here, it is going to stay and it is going to grow larger. Moreover, it will only become more unavoidable as the century progresses. Though few issues seem to be pricklier for high-income countries, good management of migration *is* possible. It is managed with varying degrees of success all across high-income countries. However, it requires something that most countries are not particularly good at: the ability to think and act across the whole of government. And when it comes to integration issues, it also requires the engagement of the whole of society, a rarity everywhere.

This essay argues that the shrinking pool of workers and consumers, a quickly ageing population, and the resulting negative demographic momentum raise crucial questions about the future of many of Europe's high-income countries. Specifically, it is about who will do the work, who will pay the taxes needed to support the dense social infrastructures of European societies, and who will buy the products and services that European firms produce? One option is getting more out of the existing population by raising labour productivity and increasing the labour force participation rates. Another option is to increase fertility. Part of the answer must also lie with increasing intra-EU mobility and strategically selecting and attracting more workers and consumers from Europe's neighbourhood regions.

2.2 KEY OBSERVATIONS

The economic importance of migration will continue to grow for both sending and receiving countries. In the next decade or so, total migration towards high-income countries will likely grow only modestly as these countries increasingly focus on selective migration, a further curtailing of family migration, and an ever more systematic redirecting of asylum flows. The combined effect of sputtering economies and continuing fiscal woes, with their enormous overhangs of unemployed and underemployed workers (and especially the massive unemployment of young persons), suggest that unemployment and social unrest are likely to last for most of this decade.

However, this does not mean less global migration. Any slack in migration to high-income countries will be picked up with ever-increasing intensity by medium-income countries, first and foremost by the 'BRIC' plus', which includes Turkey, Mexico, South Africa and Indonesia. These countries are already large, in some instances very large, immigration players. In the next two decades, these and other fast-growing countries will become the true immigration hubs. If Turkey, for example, manages its political portfolio well, it is likely to become not only a fast-rising medium-income country, but also an attractive destination for immigration.

2.3   THE DEMOGRAPHIC LANDSCAPE: A TRIPLE-SQUEEZE

Demographic shortfalls caused by persistently low fertility rates have encouraged many European countries – including the Netherlands – to focus on migration policy and future migration trends. Low fertility rates will soon lead to shrinking pools of workers and consumers and faster-ageing populations. Together, these two trends threaten to create a negative demographic momentum, as an ever-smaller number of women of child-bearing age produce fewer children than are needed to support health and pay-as-you-go retirement systems. The persistent economic crisis will only exacerbate these trends and their effects.

The Netherlands, though, is an outlier, since its people are already older than in most other European countries and much older than countries on the other side of the Atlantic (Figure 2.1). In 2005, the median age in the Netherlands was about 39 years old, and the old age dependency ratio – the ratio of the population of 65 years and older to the population aged between 20 and 64 years — stood at about 21 per cent, which means that there are approximately five persons of working age for each individual over age 65. The old age dependency ratio and average age are predicted to rise significantly over the next two decades. In 2030, when many countries will be very old – in a few countries including Japan and Germany, the median will be about 50 years old – the median age in the Netherlands is going to be about 44 years old. The dependency ratio will also have increased to approximately 41 per cent (Table 2.1).

These three trends of shrinking pools of workers and consumers, faster-ageing populations and a resulting negative demographic momentum raise crucial questions about the future of high-income countries. Who will do the work that vibrant economies require? Who will pay the taxes needed to

Figure 2.1   Increasing dependency ratios

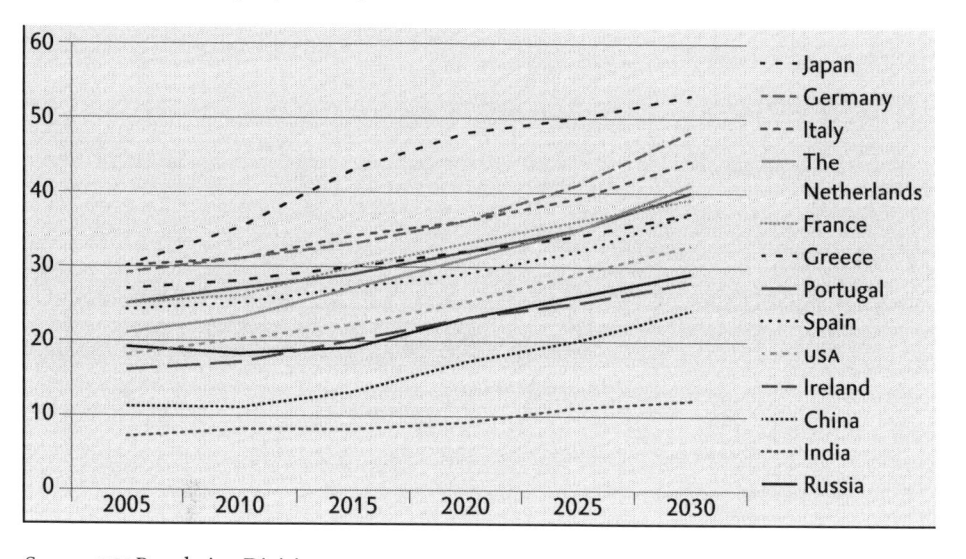

Source: UN Population Division, 2010.

Table 2.1   The demographic 'Triple Squeeze'

Country	Total fertility rate (children per woman) in 2005-2010	Median age of population 2005	Old-age dependency ratio in 2005	Old-age dependency ratio in 2030	Median age of population 2030 (projected)
Japan	1.32	43.1	30	53	51.4
Germany	1.36	42.1	29	48	48.8
The Netherlands	1.74	38.8	21	41	44.3
France	1.97	38.9	25	39	42.4
Greece	1.46	39.8	27	37	47.4
Spain	1.41	38.8	24	37	48.0
Poland	1.32	36.6	19	35	44.9
Russia	1.44	37.3	19	29	43.3
United States	2.07	36.2	18	33	39.1
China	1.64	32.2	11	24	42.5
India	2.61	23.9	7	12	31.2

Source: UN, World Population Prospects: The 2010 revision.

Table 2.2   The demography of the EU's 'Neighbourhood'

Country	Population	Median age	Population growth rate	Total fertility children/woman	Labour force
Balkans					
Albania	2,994,667	30.4 years	0.267%	1.48	1.06 million
Bosnia & Herzegovina	4,622,163	40.7 years	0.008%	-	2.60 million
Bulgaria	7,093,635	41.9 years	-0.781%	1.42	2.50 million
Croatia	4,483,804	41.4 years	-0.076%	1.43	1.76 million
Kosovo	1,825,632	26.7 years	-	-	310,000
Macedonia	2,077,328	35.8 years	0.248%	1.58	949,300
Montenegro	661,807	37.8 years	-0.705%	-	259,100
Serbia	7,310,555	41.3 years	-0.467%	-	2.95 million
East of EU					
Belarus	9,577,552	39 years	-0.363%	1.26	5.00 million
Moldova	4,314,377	35.4 years	-0.072%	1.29	1.20 million
Ukraine	45,134,707	39.9 years	-0.622%	1.28	22.02 million
North Africa & Turkey					
Algeria	34,994,937	27.6 years	1.173%	1.75	10.81 million
Egypt	82,079,636	24.3 years	1.96%	2.97	26.20 million
Libya	6,597,960	24.5 years	2.064%	2.96	1.73 million
Morocco	31,968,361	26.9 years	1.067%	2.21	11.63 million
Tunisia	10,629,186	30 years	0.978%	2.03	3.829 million
Turkey	78,785,548	28.5 years	1.235%	2.15	25.64 million

Source: CIA World Factbook 2011.

support the dense social infrastructure that is one of Europe's signal achievements? Who will buy the products and services that European firms produce?

One possibility is to get more out of the existing population by adjusting domestic and EU-wide policy to identify groups that are socially and economically marginalised (and, as a result, deeply under-represented in the labour force) and to work hard to incorporate them. But regardless of how successful such policies might be, more policy adjustments will be required. These will have to include adjustments to retirement and pensions, by raising the retirement age, trimming benefits, and closing the time gap between when people stop working (whether voluntarily or not) and when pensions become available.

Getting more out of people also means increasing employment rates by raising the labour participation rates of women, minorities, older workers, and immigrants and their offspring through positive (affirmative) measures *and* through the tactical use of social supports (both incentives and disincentives). In addition, governments should think much harder about part-time work by, for instance, restructuring part-time work to fit the talent pool, offering tax concessions and incentives to employers so that they offer workers training and benefits, and assisting those part-time workers who want to get into full-time jobs to do so.

Another possibility is to continue efforts to increase fertility. France, Germany, Greece, many Nordic countries, Japan and Korea and many others have explicit, even aggressive, pro-natalist policies. However, the results of such policies are very mixed.

Increasingly, part of the answer will also lie with increasing intra-EU mobility. This has been accelerating already, and the European Commission is preparing

Figure 2.2   Working-age population (15-64 year-olds) in MENA sending*, the EU27, and select MENA sending countries

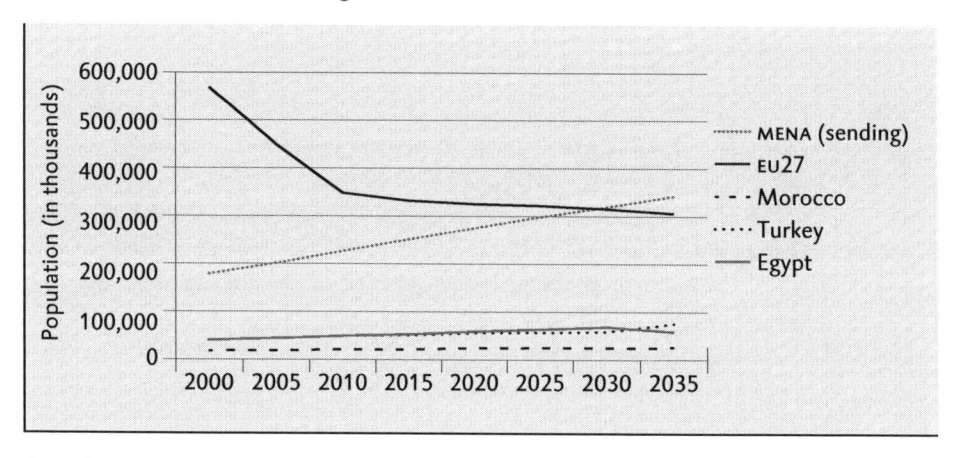

* For the purposes of this chart, MENA sending countries are: Algeria, Egypt, Iraq, Jordan, Lebanon, Morocco, Sudan, Syria, Tunisia, Turkey & Yemen
Source: UNDP World Population Prospects 2010 (latest as of 2012)

Figure 2.3 New workers in the EU and the MENA*region

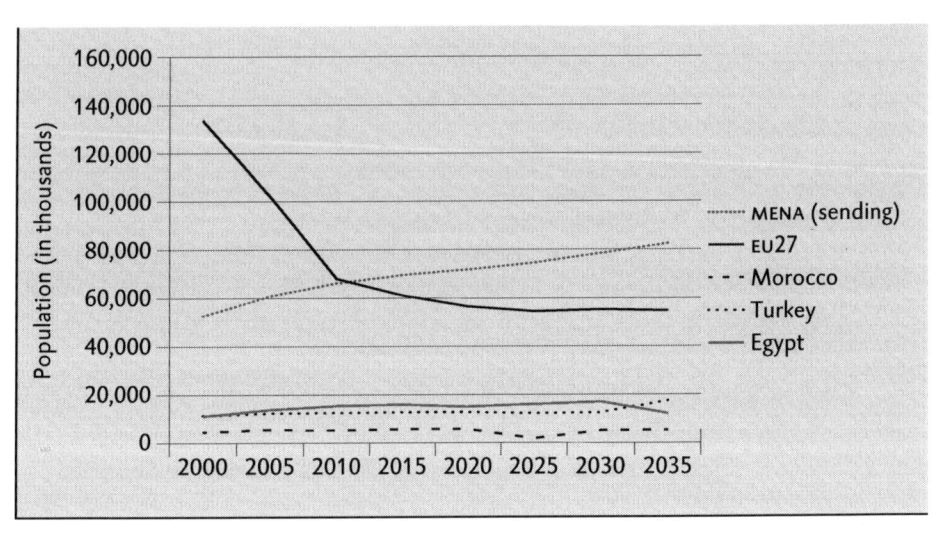

* For the purposes of this chart, MENA sending countries are: Algeria, Egypt, Iraq, Jordan, Lebanon, Morocco, Sudan, Syria, Tunisia, Turkey and Yemen
Source: UNDP World Population Prospects 2010 (latest as of 2012)

financial incentives to facilitate it further. Finally, another part of the answer will lie with attracting more workers/consumers from Europe's neighbourhood. After all, migration is first and foremost a neighbourhood affair. Neither the Balkans, nor the countries immediately east of the EU provide much of an answer though, because their demographic profiles are very similar to the EU's profile (see Table 2.2). The Middle East and North Africa (MENA) region, however, holds a much greater demographic promise (Figures 2.2 and 2.3). Yet it also brings enormous political baggage.

2.4 PREPARING INTELLIGENTLY FOR MORE MIGRATION

How can governments and receiving societies prepare intelligently for more migration? Openings to migration are always difficult. Hence, all players must do their part. Government must build legal frameworks for the entry, employment, and integration of migrants; attend carefully to security issues, including managing immigration's 'back door'; and experiment with various types of migration in order to come up with the right mix. The business community must also step up to the plate and allow firms to select the foreign workers they need (just as they do with all other workers), but also expect them to train and help such workers advance without either positive or negative discrimination. And civil society must hold both government and business accountable for how they treat migrants; work with them on developing, defining and implementing integration programmes; and advocate aggressively for all marginalised populations.

Thinking strategically about the future also requires viewing the Mediterranean and North Africa (MENA) region as a partner and an economic resource. This suggests that Europe should invest intelligently in building up the region's human capital stocks – a strategy that gives workers and their families opportunities for growth, builds up local economic opportunities, creates growing classes of consumers, and, for those who will migrate, enables them to do better for themselves *and simultaneously offer greater value to their employers and the community of which they become part.* Only then can today's sorry narrative about migration in Europe be rewritten.

Furthermore, Europe should open its markets and create a safe and secure environment for investment in the MENA region under preferential tariff rules until a customs union or, at minimum, proper free trade and investment agreements are negotiated and come into force. Lastly, Europe should create incentives for firms to relocate some of their production facilities to the region as a means of creating more job opportunities there (and eventually, markets) and reducing labour demand in the continent as the supply of youth begins to shrink.

2.5   COMPETING FOR THE BEST AND THE BRIGHTEST

In addition to preparing for more managed migration to overcome demographic deficits, European governments must also prepare to become more competitive in attracting the better skilled workers robust economies require. The rationale is clear. Although the immigrant pipeline will remain strong for the next two decades, the supply of skilled migrants will not. But well before the supply of skilled migrants begins to dry up, competition for these migrants will increase as the BRIC plus and other fast-growing countries begin fishing in the same talent pool as high-income countries do now.

If much of future migration to high-income countries is thus likely to be selective or highly selective, the question for high-income countries becomes how to attract and keep the best immigrants. Or to put it more provocatively: how will *they* (skilled immigrants) choose where to go?

In many ways, the easy part of immigration policymaking relates to the highly skilled and the very highly skilled – the best and the brightest. Most countries create points systems that rate prospective immigrants on education, income, job offers or scarce professions. A growing minority of countries, however,

including Sweden, Norway and, of course, the United States, allow employers to recruit workers from abroad directly according to set parameters. In the
Netherlands and Austria, elements of these two models are combined into a
hybrid system that simplifies how to deal with the immigration of the highly
skilled. Such a system also allows firms to choose more naturally the medium-
skilled workers that many firms need. It also reduces the pressure on government to define how many immigrant workers the economy may need, and
allows it to focus on the more important questions of managing the overall
migration system within the context of crucial reforms to the education and
social policy systems.

What all of the recruitment schemes do not account for, however, is that the key
question will increasingly become not how we will choose the best migrants,
but how migrants will choose us. Research, interviews and collaboration with
people in both the sending and receiving countries provides evidence of a fairly
simple set of variables influencing migrants' choices of destination (Figure
2.4). The first-tier variables are the most important from the perspective of
the would-be immigrant, while the second-tier variables are still important, if
less so. The third tier of variables relates to the immigration system itself and is

Figure 2.4   Variables influencing migrants' choices of destination

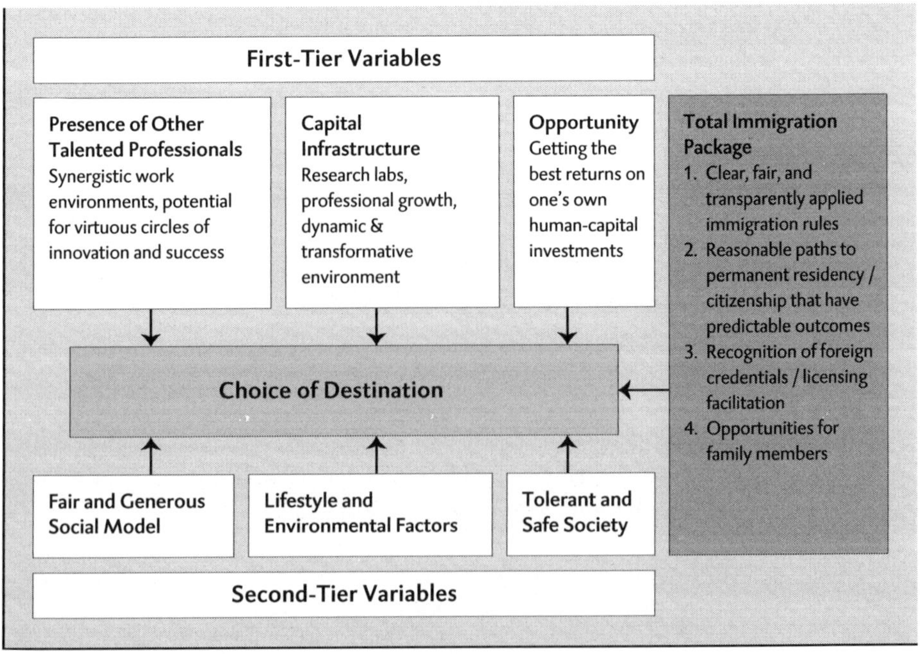

Source: Papademetriou, Migration Policy Institute 2012.

one that smart governments can manipulate most easily in order to make their country more appealing to prospective immigrants.

The first tier consists of variables that governments can do something about, but it does require large investments. Talented professionals want to work with other talented professionals. Attracting talent requires capital to create an infrastructure of universities, research labs and private-public sector arrangements that can, in turn, create multiplier effects. It also needs to create opportunity for personal advancement, a prerequisite that gives a prohibitive advantage to the United States.

Second-tier variables like a fair and generous social system and an attractive lifestyle and environment are more difficult to influence. A tolerant and safe society, however, can be influenced by government policy. Thus, it is appropriate to ask whether some European countries still offer safe and tolerant settings, or whether government policies may have undone some of these countries' reputation among would-be immigrants from outside Europe.

Finally, the third tier of variables is what may be called the 'total immigration package'. Before they move, people want to see that there is a transparent and fair immigration system. Regardless of their status, immigrants need to know with absolute certainty and predictability what the rules are, including the rules for citizenship. Whether immigrants can bring their families and under what circumstances, is also an important consideration when choosing a destination country. Finally, foreign credentials need to be readily and fairly recognised.

2.6   ANXIETY ABOUT IMMIGRATION: TWO KEY GOVERNANCE CHALLENGES

As global migration has increased, so too has anxiety about immigration. Its main roots lie in the speed with which immigration has grown, which has fuelled natural anxieties about social and cultural change and brought to the fore national identity insecurities and apprehensions. Adding to this anxiety is the fact that many (and in some cases *most*) new immigrants come from countries of large social, cultural and ethnic 'distances'. In recent years, religious distance has often seemed to take 'pride of place' among these differences and has defined much of the anxiety. Finally, the increasing 'visibility' and 'otherness' of some newcomers fuels discomfort among host populations and shapes their reactions to immigration. These and related issues frame a significant part of the governance challenge most high-income countries have faced with immigration.

Two such challenges are important to mention. The first is integrating immigrants into society. All too frequently some immigrant groups and their offspring lag well behind natives with regard to language ability, educational achievement, access to opportunity (employment, earnings, quality of housing), and social and political engagement. The fiscal crisis and lingering economic weakness exacerbate these differences. The on-the-ground effect of these disparities is the building up of *cumulative disadvantage* (expressing itself in varying forms and degrees of economic, social and political marginalisation) and the breeding of mutual wariness. The result is that many immigrant communities feel aggrieved, while many natives view immigrants and their children with impatience, if not mistrust and suspicion.

The second governance challenge is controlling illegal immigration *and* resisting the irresponsible growth of immigration. The essence of success on migration is managing an orderly and flexibly regulated flow of legal immigrants. But managing legal migration well may not be enough either to turn the tables on gaining more from migration or on how immigration is perceived in many countries. To do so requires two additional things. First, it requires success in controlling illegal immigration (the US is the 'poster child' of failure in this regard – although things may be changing). Second, it requires maintaining a sense of measure in how to grow a legal immigration flow (Spain is the poster child of how *not* to do so). Good management and legality serve the interests of most immigration actors well, except those of the criminal syndicates that move people, unscrupulous employers, family networks that ignore laws with relative impunity, the 'migration facilitation industry', and oblivious or completely self-interested consumers.

2.7   CONCLUSION

In today's globalised world, Europe's high-income countries are facing demographic decline and will increasingly compete for skilled migrants. However, the speed at which migration rates have increased and the mixed or even poor track records of governments' integration policies over the past two decades have understandably fuelled anxiety about migration across societies. As a result, governments need to redouble their efforts and address successfully a double governance challenge: investing intelligently in immigrant integration to promote upward mobility, and managing an orderly and flexibly regulated flow of legal migrants while strictly controlling illegal migration.

NOTES

1   BRIC stands for: Brazil, Russia, India and China

3   SATISFYING LABOUR NEEDS IN AN AGEING SOCIETY[1]

Georges Lemaître

3.1   INTRODUCTION

The demographic change that is underway in almost all OECD countries – the retirement of the large baby boom cohorts and their replacement by smaller youth cohorts – has many policymakers concerned. Governments are accustomed to dealing with economic growth in the context of demographic expansion, but addressing demographic contraction seems like a different game. There are fears among national and international policymakers (European Commission 2009) that there will not be enough workers or enough of the right kinds of workers to replace those who will be retiring. Implicit in these fears is the belief that demand will persist and that even if many business owners retire, their businesses will not necessarily 'retire' with them. There will be a continued need for workers to satisfy the labour needs of enterprises in order for them to maintain their level of activity, let alone to expand. Also hovering in the background is the concern that the increase in social expenditures as a result of the pension and health care financing requirements for retired persons will put a strain on public budgets, which would be exacerbated by lessened contributions from a smaller workforce. There is an underlying assumption here as well, which is that the other sources of additional economic activity, namely increased productivity growth, additional hours of work and increases in participation rates will not be enough to offset the expected decline in the size of the working-age population or to provide or compensate for the types of skills that will be needed by enterprises. Recourse to increased labour migration thus seems inevitable.

For these reasons, the question of future labour and skill needs and how these are to be identified and satisfied is prominent on the radar screen of policymakers. But cannot the labour market be expected to adjust to satisfy the needs of employers? It can, and it will no doubt do so, but one means of adjustment is precisely the recruitment of labour from outside the country and this currently is not a freely available option to employers, they way, for example, other options are, such as wage adjustments, overtime, new technology, outsourcing or moving production abroad. There are externalities associated with opening up migration, among them the longer-term costs and benefits of migration to societies and the constraints imposed by public opinion, which employers may not take into account but which governments cannot ignore. In practice, this means that labour migration is and will no doubt continue to be more constrained than other means of adjustment and that domestic means of satisfying labour needs will generally have priority, among governments if not always necessarily among employers. Parenthetically, filling labour needs through domestic sources has one advantage which recruitment from abroad does not, namely it maintains or increases production without adding to the population and to societal costs.

3.2   DEMOGRAPHIC CHANGE, THE EVOLUTION OF THE LABOUR MARKET AND THE RESPONSE OF LABOUR MIGRATION POLICY

Scenarios concerning the impact of ageing on the labour market are often phrased in terms of the effect on the working-age population (European Commission 2009), which is projected to decline in Europe by about 2.5 per cent by 2020 and by almost 6.5 per cent by 2030 (by 1.7% and 6.0% resp. for the Netherlands), *at current migration levels.*[2] The implication is that this decline must be offset and that there will be a need for new workers, including migrants, to move into the occupations from which older workers are retiring. The picture, however, is not so simple.

First of all, in many countries, participation is increasing and workers are prolonging their working lives, which increases the size of the labour force. Second, the labour market participation of young cohorts is higher than that of older ones, which will help counterbalance the decline in the size of youth cohorts. Third, the generational occupational replacement model is not an entirely reliable one, because the labour market is dynamic and occupations are changing. One cannot think narrowly of labour needs in terms of persons needed to replace retiring workers. Over the 2000-2010 decade, for example (Figure 3.1), there were almost three times as many entries into strongly growing occupations in Europe by youth alone as there were retirements from these and almost one and one half times as many retirements from strongly declining occupations as there were youth and new immigrant entries combined (OECD 2012a).[3] In other words, jobs in some occupations are not replaced but rather cut when their incumbents retire. In other occupations, there is nothing to replace; the jobs are new ones, few of which existed before.

Over the decade, significant numbers of immigrant entries were observed in both growing and declining occupations, but the immigrant numbers were a fraction of the total movements into these occupations (Table 3.1). If 2000-2010 is any indication, large numbers of workers retiring from an occupation do not necessarily imply that many immigrants will have to be recruited to make up for the (apparent) shortfall in youth entries, nor does a significant inflow of

Figure 3.1   Contributions to occupational change by source and occupational growth quintile, 2000-2010 (in thousands).

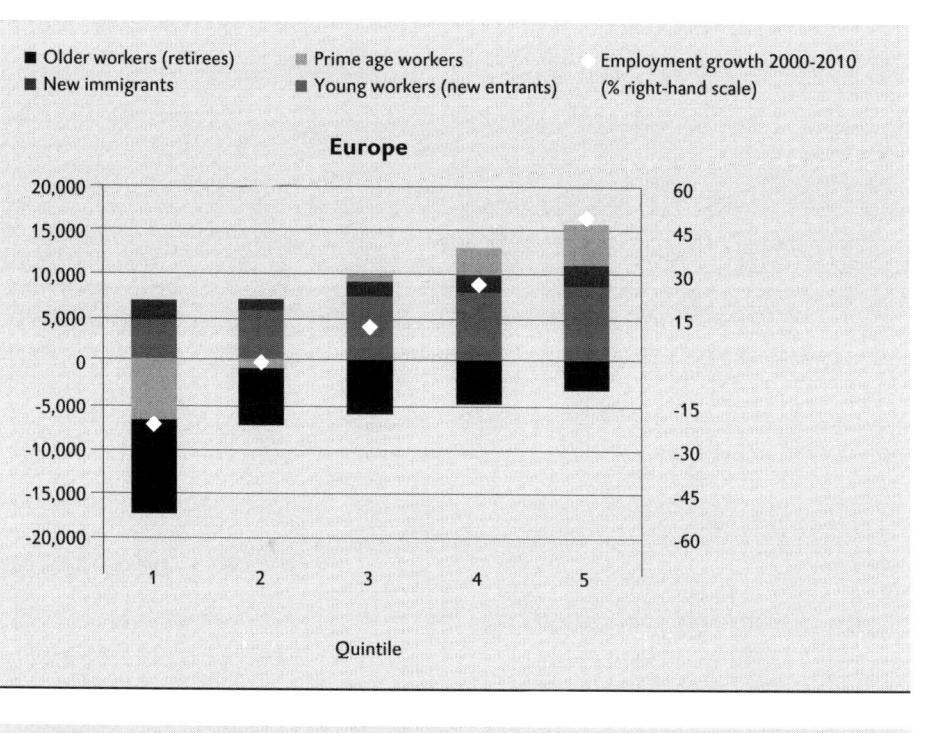

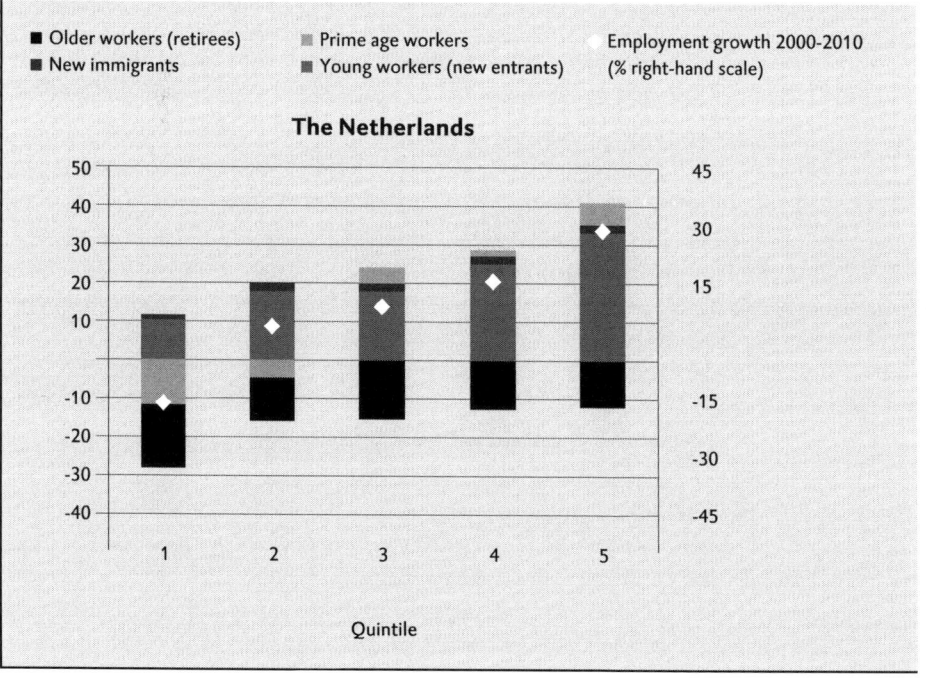

Table 3.1   Rate of replacement/expansion of occupations, by source and occupational growth quintile, 2000-2010.

	Europe		The Netherlands	
	By domestic sources	By immigrants	By domestic sources	By immigrants
Growth quintile	(percentages)			
1	25	8	37	4
2	77	13	113	11
3	137	23	144	16
4	225	37	209	16
5	465	64	323	15
All occupations	108	19	123	10

resident youth into strongly growing occupations obviate the need for recruitment from abroad. Recruitment needs will depend on the precise nature of labour demand, which seems difficult to predict over the medium term. What role is international labour migration then to play in the context of an ageing workforce? If one were to specify the objective of labour migration policy, it is likely that a consensus view would yield something like the following, namely, to satisfy those labour market needs which cannot be filled from within the country in a timely fashion and at reasonable cost, without having adverse effects on the domestic workforce. But this is not an objective which is specific to an ageing context. It applies whatever the economic conditions. And it concerns all skill levels, not just the highly skilled. The question is whether anything more needs to be done because of the particularities of the ageing context, namely shortages arising out of significant demographic imbalances in the workforce.

3.3   THE IDENTIFICATION OF LABOUR NEEDS

Historically, labour migration policy has been focused on current labour needs and this is likely to be the case as well in the context of ageing, at least in the first instance. In practice, this means relying on requests from employers as the initial means of identifying shortages.[4] This statement is somewhat ingenuous, however, in that there have almost always been constraints imposed upstream by governments on the nature of jobs for which labour migration is allowed, in the form of minimum educational qualifications or wage thresholds or oc-cupations for which recruitment is allowed. For example, in many countries, permanent labour migration for low-skilled jobs has been extremely limited, because such jobs were considered relatively easy to fill from the domestic labour market.

Now governments have rarely relied exclusively on declarations of employ-ers as a fully reliable indicator of labour shortages. There is therefore often a verification process required of recruitment requests, which may involve a test of the local labour market by the employer for possible candidates or an assess-ment of local labour market conditions by public employment agencies. There is also generally a requirement that wages and working conditions be according to domestic standards, because of a desire to protect domestic workers from potentially damaging competition.

The labour market test or assessment is often waived for occupations which are deemed to be in shortage. Indeed, in a growing number of OECD countries, in anticipation of the shortages expected due to ageing, the test or assessment is waived with respect to recruitment of highly skilled labour migrants in general, essentially because high-skilled occupations are those showing the strongest growth, because highly educated immigrants are deemed to contribute posi-tively to the economy, and because, even in high-skilled occupations where there are no shortages, highly educated residents are considered to be equipped to compete effectively with immigrants for available jobs. Most countries have also introduced measures to facilitate the stay after graduation of international students who are able to find work commensurate with their studies, with no need for employers to test the labour market for domestic applicants.[5]

Is there anything more that governments need to do to ensure that immigra-tion is able to supply the needed workers who cannot be found in the domestic labour market? Current levels of even highly skilled migration in many coun-tries are, after all, relatively low and this is sometimes interpreted as a sign of the unattractiveness of certain countries to immigrants, for which govern-ments, it is argued, have to introduce incentives. In addition, future needs are expected to be large and to involve many sectors of the economy and establish-ments of all sizes, many of which may never have recruited from abroad.

Population ageing, however, is only just starting. As of 2010, about 40 per cent of the baby boom cohort of workers born between 1945 and 1954 was retired. And in many European countries in the period just prior to the recession (2005-2008), increases in employment came largely from increases in the em-ployment rates of residents rather than from the employment of new immi-grants, whether arriving for work or for other reasons (OECD 2010). This was

Figure 3.2   Contributions to changes in occupational skill levels, by demographic group, 2000-2010.

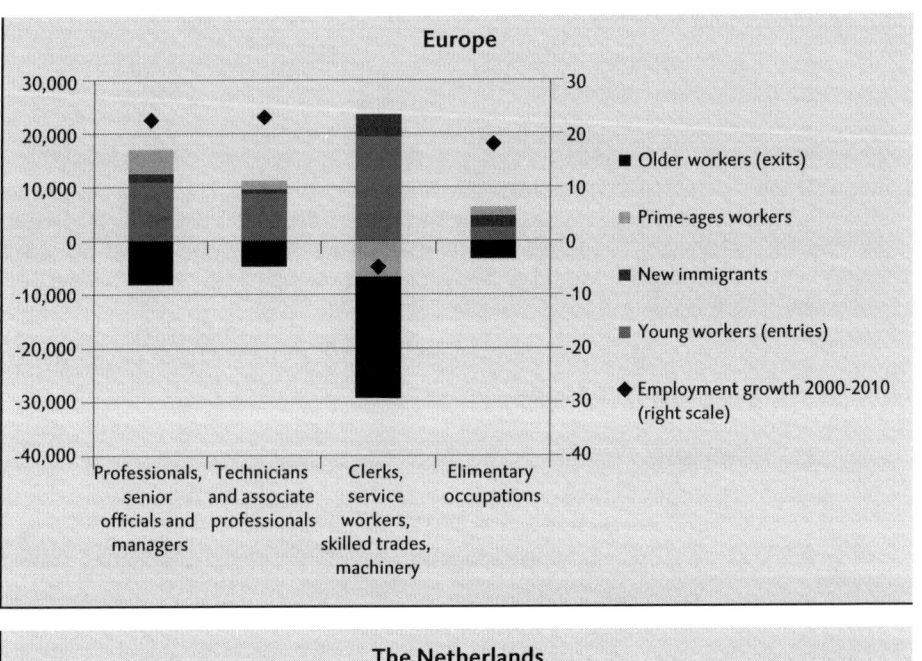

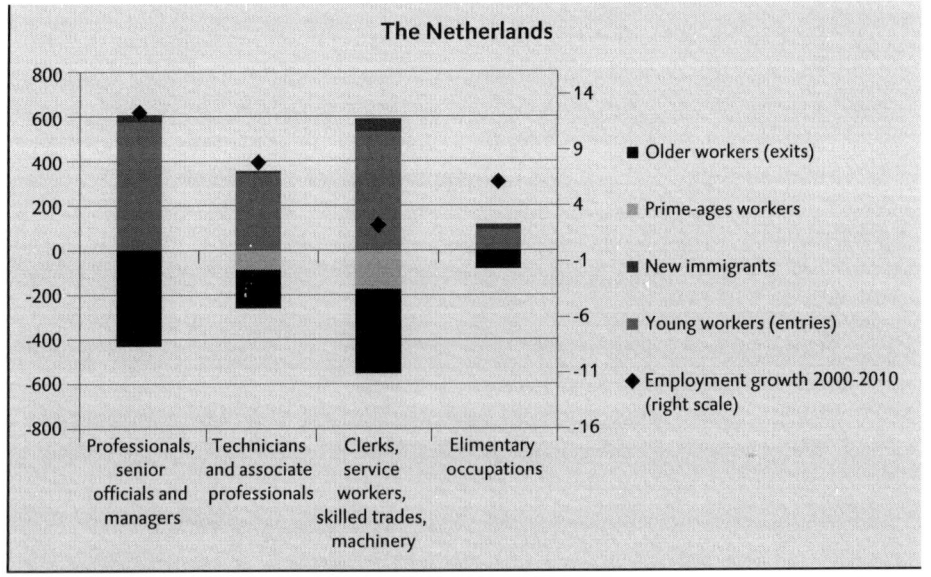

even the case in countries such as Germany and Japan, where demographic change is more advanced than in most countries,[6] and in Switzerland and Denmark, where employment rates of residents were already very high. It was also the case in the Netherlands. There is clearly some potential for mobilising the domestic workforce in many countries and this, along with the crisis, could explain the restrained demand for immigrant workers thus far.

The domestic potential, however, is not unlimited and in countries which have been less affected by the crisis, such as Australia and Canada, demographic pressures are starting to make themselves felt more strongly, and over all segments of the skills spectrum, not just the highly skilled. This is likely to be the case in Europe too. Growth in employment over the last decade has occurred not only in high-skilled jobs but also in so-called elementary occupations, which consist of the lowest skilled jobs (Figure 3.2). It is rather among medium-skilled jobs that employment has declined, although not in the Netherlands, where – as elsewhere – they have grown more slowly than high- and low-skilled jobs.

The Swedish Example

One country which has opted for an open, demand-driven system, with few restrictions, is Sweden. The Swedish model is a particularly interesting one, because it illustrates how a relatively open migration system can operate in practice, with the initiative for recruitment from abroad being entirely in the hands of employers.

The new labour migration system introduced in Sweden in December 2008 assumes that employers are the best placed to know whether a recruitment from abroad is justified (OECD 2011). The position to be recruited for must be advertised for two weeks prior to the request, but there is no requirement that the employer interview domestic applicants for the job. The wages and working conditions specified in the job offer must be according to domestic standards, as is the case in most countries for recruitment from abroad. In Sweden labour unions are asked to review the wages and working conditions offered. The underlying assumption is that, under this set of constraints, employers will normally prefer domestic candidates, among others for reasons of language proficiency, familiarity with Swedish work practices and cheaper recruitment costs. Except for special recruitment channels involving, among others, international students and rejected asylum seekers, the labour migration regime in Sweden involves essentially recruitment of workers from abroad, with the additional costs and delays which this implies relative to domestic recruitment.

Recruitment costs, however, are not the only economic factor at play in recruitment. The returns on moving to an OECD country are high for immigrants from a developing country and involve the benefits of a lifetime of residence, not just the immediate benefits of higher wages and better living conditions after arrival. Some immigrants may be willing – or may be pressured by less scrupulous employers who are seeking workers – to give way on wages and working conditions in the short term in return for the longer-term benefits for them and their families of living in Sweden. In other words, there are ways to abuse the system.

Sweden also has a shortage occupation list and although this list has little bearing on the occupations for which recruitment is allowed, over fifty per cent of recruitment under the new labour migration regime has been in occupations for which there are no ostensible shortages, many of them low-skilled. Although there has been an increase in recruitment for low-skilled jobs in Sweden (from 9% of recruitments under the old system to 16% under the new), recruitments overall have not exploded and only exceeded pre-recession totals in 2011 (excluding seasonal work). Still, there is some suspicion that not all job offers may be legitimate or that signed contracts may not always reflect the original offers transmitted to the Swedish Migration Board. Administrative procedures have been put in place in Sweden to ensure a better identification of questionable requests and better follow-up of work contract arrangements following arrival. Verification and enforcement are costly, but they are an essential guarantee of a viable labour migration system in the face of possible abuse and an often sceptical public opinion.[7]

Is the Swedish labour migration regime a model for other countries? It is clear that it is not easily transferable elsewhere. The union review of job offers may not be possible in countries where collective bargaining coverage is less extensive than in Sweden and the administrative data system in Sweden provides tools to aid in the review of recruitment requests which may not be available in other countries. But it does demonstrate that a relatively open system, with appropriate safeguards in place, need not result in flows which are out of control.

Occupational Shortage Lists
In some countries, governments go to the trouble of identifying, upstream, occupations for which shortages exist and for these, labour migration is allowed and/or facilitated. This eliminates the need for a test of the local labour market, but the shortage occupation list needs to be regularly updated to take account of changing labour market conditions and the effect of recent recruitments. Note that the list approach need not – indeed, should not – exclude the possibility of recruitment for occupations not on the list. The identification of shortage occupations is not an exact science and the possibility that there may be shortages locally or in specialised occupations that are not on the list should be allowed for.[8]

Can countries rely entirely on employer-driven requests for foreign labour as the barometer of labour needs that must be satisfied from abroad? Or are these likely to be greater, because employers cannot find the workers or the skills which they need? Recruitment from abroad has generally been the preserve of large companies with foreign contacts and clients, and for whom recourse to recruitment agencies or agents is often a routine matter. The same cannot necessarily be said for small and medium-sized enterprises, for whom recruitment 'off the street' may be the more usual procedure and whose labour needs may be more at the medium and lower ends of the skills spectrum, where offshore recruitment is less common. Indeed, irregular migration and employment may well be fostered by the fact that for low-skilled jobs, it is difficult for formal recruitment from abroad to compete with hiring 'off the street'. This is why procedures for such recruitment have to be relatively expeditious, while strict monitoring and follow-up of recruitments are necessary to ensure that abuses are kept to a minimum.

Sweden does allow for the possibility of potential immigrants coming to Sweden to search for work (on a special visa) or for persons coming to Sweden for a job interview to 'shop around' while they are in Sweden, but only for jobs in occupations which are on the national occupational shortage list. This possibility, however, is rarely used, accounting for less than one per cent of recruitment over the first two and a half years of that the new Swedish labour migration regime was in effect.

Experience in Sweden suggests that employers have little trouble identifying and recruiting workers for low-skilled jobs, whether because they use recruitment agencies, because they identify potential labour migrants abroad through current immigrant employees, or indeed because the employers are themselves immigrants with extensive contacts in their countries of origin.[9] In other countries, in particular Korea and Spain, anonymous lists of pre-screened potential immigrants are established in collaboration with public employment services in the countries of origin with which the destination country has signed bilateral agreements (OECD 2009). These pre-screened lists, however, concern only applicants for low- to medium-skilled jobs, for which Internet recruitment, for example, is not (yet) common. This approach implies that certain countries of origin are favoured in the process, since destination countries cannot have a presence in every country of origin. Better co-ordination in organising migration movements may result, since agreements can be revoked if there are widespread abuses.

Difficulties in identifying and recruiting appropriate higher skilled migrants may be more problematical, if the skills needed are difficult to find. Language is one such skill and it is clear that the pool of potential immigrants who speak Dutch around the world is limited. However, there is no shortage of English-speakers and this can be used as a transition language in the workplace. This is undoubtedly already the case in the Dutch labour migration regime and in the Nordic countries as well but will need to be more broadly adopted as small and medium-sized enterprises where the language at work is Dutch enter the recruitment process.

Points Systems – a Selection Tool, not a Migration Regime
It is sometimes proposed that countries should adopt points systems in order to make them more attractive to potential immigrants. Points systems, however, are not a recruitment system *per se* but merely a selection tool to provide for the possibility of selecting immigrants on the basis of more than one characteristic, for example, educational attainment, age and wage level. If several selection criteria are involved, one has to weight each of them, that is, assign different points to each criterion and define an overall point threshold to determine whether an applicant will be accepted. Such points systems traditionally have been implemented in countries such as Australia, Canada and New Zealand, under whose migration system candidates were not required to have a job offer in order to be eligible for immigration (with their families). But points systems have also been implemented more recently in regimes which depend on a job offer, such as in the United Kingdom Tier 2 system. They also provide more flexibility in identifying appropriate candidates, who can be highly skilled without necessarily having, for example, a university qualification.

Points systems may have a certain aura because of their association with migration regimes such as Canada's, which are generally viewed as successful ones, but this is about the only sense in which they can contribute to country attractiveness. They can be a useful tool in screening potential migrants, but are complementary to job offers to employers. Indeed, Australia and Canada are according more and more importance to job offers in their points systems, because outcomes for immigrants selected under the points system without a job offer have not been as good in those countries as used to be case in the past.

The emerging need for low- and medium-skilled workers in Canada has given rise to the Provincial Nominee Programme (PNP), a labour migration programme in which the normal selection criteria at the national levels are waived and provinces take responsibility for the selection and screening of workers for immigration, on the basis of job offers satisfying a number of criteria related to wages, working conditions and occupational category. Provincial nominees then apply at the national level for health and security clearance and for evaluation of their language proficiency; those satisfying the basic requirements are admitted into Canada as permanent residents. The PNP has provided for recruitment in occupations as diverse as food and beverage production workers, hotel desk agents/clerks, many manufacturing occupations, long-haul truck drivers, and so on.

3.4   LOW-SKILLED MIGRATION

One particular concern in many countries is that there will be a need for migrants to fill low- or lesser-skilled jobs. Generally these have been filled by migrants with low educational levels, often below compulsory educational levels in the country of destination. However, the track record of many countries with respect to integrating low-educated migrants and their children has not been an overly positive one. Although low-educated migrants may be recruited directly into jobs, their long-term employability may be an issue, among other reasons because limited language proficiency and education make retraining for available jobs problematic, should they lose the ones for which they were originally recruited. In addition, their limited earnings (and capital) mean that low-skilled migrants tend to locate and concentrate in areas where housing is cheaper. In practice, this means that their children tend to be concentrated in schools where there are many children of low-income parents. Analyses have shown that school disadvantage of this kind compounds parental educational disadvantage, for all children, whatever their origin, but especially for immigrant children (OECD 2012b). Indeed social segregation and its consequences on the outcomes of the children of migrants is undoubtedly one of the most difficult issues which destination countries have had and continue to face. To a great extent, the fact that most countries prefer that low-skilled migration remain temporary is an admission, if not of failure, then at least that solutions are difficult to find and implement.

Can one ensure that temporary migrants remain temporary? Incentives can be introduced for both employers and migrants which encourage 'temporariness', and enforcement of stay requirements can be stepped up. Requiring employers to post bonds or withholding immigrant social security contributions to be disbursed as a lump-sum payment upon their return to their country of origin are examples of such incentives. Many low-skilled labour needs, however, are not temporary and in such cases, both employers and immigrants have an incentive to maintain the employment relationship. Indeed, experience in a number of countries has shown that in situations where migrants have been granted temporary permits for jobs which are ongoing, it is employers who lobby, often successfully, to relax the rules, either to allow a renewal of the permit or a readmission after a brief return to the home country. In any event, without permanent recruitment, structural low-skilled needs would accumulate over time, which would require larger and larger temporary movements to keep up with the demand, a situation which would not be sustainable. In short, it seems likely that low-skilled labour needs may well develop that cannot be filled from domestic sources of labour supply or from temporary labour migration and that recruitment from abroad will need to take place.

Prospects for Lesser-Skilled Labour Migration

Many countries are not optimistic about their and immigrants' abilities to achieve favourable labour market outcomes over the longer term *on average*, as well as educational and labour outcomes for their children. Note the emphasis on 'on average'. Every country can point to success stories among the children of poorly educated immigrated parents – poor outcomes are not inevitable – but the argument here concerns the average, and there is little question that, on average, children of low-educated immigrants generally do not fare well in OECD countries, especially when concentrated in disadvantaged schools. In addition to the above, there is also a concern that low-skilled migration will give rise to further waves of low-educated chain migration of family members and marriage partners, resulting in a further deterioration of outcomes.

One unspoken assumption concerning the lesser-skilled jobs in question is that labour needs for such jobs would be filled by the same kind of migrants whose outcomes and whose children's outcomes policy has been less than successful at addressing in the past. But this has sometimes involved migration of persons of very low educational levels, often below compulsory educational levels in OECD countries. Would this necessarily persist with employer-driven recruitment for lower-skilled jobs? Educational attainment levels have been rising in sending countries, and employers can be expected to have a preference for better educated workers if they are recruiting abroad. In addition, migration policy can clearly lay down some standards and requirements.

Minimum Educational Requirements?

One such requirement concerns a minimum educational level for labour migrants. In many countries this is already in place, but trivially so, in that labour migration is restricted to highly educated workers. This restriction is likely to drop with the emergence of shortages in lesser-skilled jobs, for which the question of minimum educational levels can be legitimately raised. All countries normally require a minimum number of years of schooling of everyone born in the country or arriving when young, whether or not they eventually enter the labour force. A priori, there seems no obvious reason why labour migrants should be exempt from this requirement. Such minimum standards are intended to ensure that everyone has the minimum educational level considered necessary to function in society and the economy. Although migrants may not actually need the minimum level of education to work in the job for which they have been recruited, it would be clearly beneficial for them to have it, for reasons related to their integration and that of their children in the host society. For the lesser-skilled occupations in the Canadian PNP, for example, provinces generally insist on at least a high school diploma (12 years of primary and secondary schooling) in order for applicants to qualify.

The argument has been advanced that if a minimum educational level were imposed on migrant workers, there would be no immigrant takers for low-skilled jobs. However, the decline in domestic takers for such jobs has as more to do with rising educational attainment among resident youth than with the lack of attractiveness of such jobs. And job attractiveness is not the only criterion that brings a worker from a sending country to an OECD country. OECD countries, with their social protection, health and educational systems and their way of life, remain attractive destinations for many residents of non-member countries. Not all countries may enjoy the reputation of certain OECD countries as destinations among potential migrant populations, but to many migrants, almost any OECD country may look like a good prospect. There is little sign that immigrants with upper secondary diplomas are shying away from lesser-skilled jobs in Canada.

One risk with regard to setting higher standards for recruits for low-skilled jobs is that employers will prefer them to low-educated residents in the labour market for the same kinds of jobs. There is some evidence, for example, that the often more highly educated immigrants who arrived in the United Kingdom from the new EU enlargement countries took on lesser skilled jobs and depressed the wages of workers at the low end of the wage spectrum (Dustmann et al. 2008). This outcome, however, was under conditions of free circulation of workers from the enlargement countries, with no government action to limit their numbers. A more cautious approach is required as labour markets open up to recruitment of workers at all skill levels from outside the EU, to ensure that domestic sources of labour supply are not driven from the labour market. Outmigration to other countries for work is not really a viable option for the latter group.

3.5   CONCLUSION - BEYOND THE ECONOMIC CRISIS

As countries edge slowly into economic recovery in these difficult times, the slack in the labour market can be expected to be absorbed and demographic imbalances to exert their influence. There remains a considerable potential for mobilising domestic labour resources in many European countries before a broader-based recourse to labour migration from outside the European Union becomes necessary. As needs become more pressing, employer demand will manifest itself and this still seems the most reliable indicator of structural labour shortages, given the difficulty of predicting these over the medium term.

Achieving the right balance between domestic means of labour adjustment and recruitment from abroad is a difficult task and requires some careful preparation, both to ensure that domestic candidates for employment get a fair chance but also that employers have sensible access to foreign recruitment for labour needs which cannot be met domestically. But governments may not get it exactly right the first time and adjustments will in any event have to be made as conditions change. Managing international migration is a complex undertaking and experience has shown that loopholes in existing regulations will be quickly exploited. More and more governments are building in administrative flexibility in migration systems, to allow for changes in response to rapidly evolving developments, without having to carry out time-consuming and politically difficult legislative reforms. The extent of labour migration to be allowed is in the end a labour market issue and treating it as such may well be the best response to addressing the political controversy to which migration in general gives rise.

NOTES

1   The opinions and arguments expressed in this chapter do not necessarily reflect the official views of the OECD or of the governments of its member countries.

2   Based on UN projections, World Population Prospects 2010, United Nations Population Division.

3   Strongly growing/declining occupations represented the top/bottom 20 per cent of 2010 employment in occupations with the highest/lowest growth rates over the period 2000 to 2010.

4   This evidently concerns employer-driven migration, in which an immigrant must have a job offer in order to immigrate. In cases where immigrants are assessed on the basis of their characteristics, preference may be given to immigrants in certain occupations, whether or not they have a job offer. This involves identifying upstream the occupations which will be favoured.

5   The growth of international study has been spurred by the proliferation of English-language programmes in many countries, which may indeed attract more international students but do not prepare them to find work in environments where the national language is the language at work.

6   The employment rate in Germany increased by fully 7 percentage points between 2000 and 2010 and those of older workers by 20 percentage points. In Japan, the working-age population decreased by 5.4 million persons over the 2000-2010 decade, but the labour force declined by less than 1.8 million persons.

7   One possible element of this is a process for certifying employers who respect the rules and for whom procedures are streamlined. This kind of process exists in the United Kingdom, for example.

8   It has been argued by some that local shortages are best addressed through inter-regional migration. Intra-national mobility, however, may be constrained by other factors, such as moving costs and the presence of family and friends.

9   How employers actually go about finding workers abroad is an topic on which precise statistical information is scarce.

REFERENCES

Dustmann, C., T. Frattini and I. Preston (2008) 'The Effect of Immigration along the Distribution of Wages', CReAM *Discussion Paper Series* 0803, Centre for Research and Analysis of Migration (CReAM), Department of Economics, University College London.

European Commission (2009) 'The 2009 Ageing Report: Economic and Budgetary Projections for the EU27 Member States (2008-2060)', *European Economy* 2. April 2009. Brussels.

OECD (2009) 'Workers Crossing Borders: A Roadmap for Managing Labour Migration' in *International Migration Outlook 2012*, OECD Publishing. http://dx.doi.org/10.1787/migr_outlook-2009-en.

OECD (2010) 'Recent Trends in International Migration' in *International Migration Outlook 2012*, OECD Publishing. http://dx.doi.org/10.1787/migr_outlook-2009-en.

OECD (2011) *'Recruiting Immigrant Workers: Sweden 2011'*, OECD Publishing. http://dx.doi.org/10.1787/9789264000000-en.

OECD (2012a) 'Renewing the Skills of Ageing Workforces : The Role of Migration' in *International Migration Outlook 2012*, OECD Publishing. http://dx.doi.org/10.1787/migr_outlook-2012-en.

OECD (2012b) 'Untapped Skills: Realising the Potential of Immigrant Students', *OECD Publishing*. http://dx.doi.org/10.1787/9789264172470-en.

4   MIGRANT WORKERS: INEVITABILITY OR POLICY CHOICE?[1]

Martin Ruhs and Bridget Anderson

4.1   INTRODUCTION

The regulation of labour immigration is one of the most important and controversial public policy issues in high-income countries. Many states in Europe and North America have experienced rapid increases in labour immigration over the past 20 years. The current global economic downturn has added further momentum to what in many countries were already highly charged debates about the impacts of rising numbers of migrants on the economic prospects of citizens and on the host economy and society more generally. A survey by the *Financial Times* in March 2009 showed that over three quarters of adults in Italy and the UK, and about two thirds in Spain, Germany, and the US, supported the idea of sending migrants who cannot find a job home (*Financial Times*, 15 March 2009).

A central question in labour immigration policy is how to link the admission of new migrant workers to the 'needs' of the domestic labour market and economy more generally. What these needs are, how they vary across sectors and occupations, and how they change during periods of economic growth and crisis are highly contested. There is significant controversy about the role that migrants can, or should, play in meeting 'skills needs' and in reducing 'labour and skills shortages' in particular sectors and occupations. Employers often claim, especially but not only during times of economic growth, that there is a 'need' for migrants to help fill labour and skills shortages and/or to do the jobs that, they allege, domestic workers will not or cannot do. Sceptics, including some trades unions, argue that in many cases these claims simply reflect employers' preference for recruiting cheap and exploitable migrant workers over improving wages and investing in the training and skills development of domestic workers. As unemployment rises, some argue, the economy's need for migrant workers declines. However, others point out there is a highly segmented labour market and a differentiated economy, suggesting that, even during times of economic downturn, new migrant workers are needed and in some occupations they may be critical to economic recovery (Finch et al. 2009).

The policy argument that immigration is required because of 'skills needs' in the domestic economy can reflect one or both of two distinct but related concerns. The first is the provision of a high level of 'human capital' in order to promote long-term economic growth and competitiveness. This line of argument is typically based on endogenous growth models that emphasise the importance of human capital, knowledge, and research and development for economic growth (see e.g. Romer 1986; Lucas 1988). Human capital models therefore suggest that the immigration of highly skilled workers is to be encouraged even without a job offer. A number of countries have labour immigration policies for admitting highly skilled migrant workers that are in part based on a human capital model, for example, Canada and Australia. Tier 1 of the UK's point-based system is an example of a labour immigration policy that is fully based on a human capital model. Such 'supply-driven' admission policies can become more difficult to politically sustain during an economic downturn. In practice, they constitute a small minority of migrant admission policies in high-income countries.

The analysis in this chapter largely focuses on a second concern that can underlie the argument that there is a 'need' for migrants' skills. This relates to the aim of using migrant workers to reduce perceived specific staff shortages which are typically expressed as labour and/or skills shortages- a highly problematic distinction as discussed further below. This type of 'shortage' argument is highly contested during both economic growth and even more so during an economic downturn. Because of the contentious nature and high policy salience of the issue, a number of countries, including Australia, Canada, and Spain, have established special government units and/or independent advisory bodies that are tasked to help link the admission of new migrant workers to research and analysis of shortages in the domestic labour market. The UK has recently established the Migration Advisory Committee (MAC), a small independent body of economists tasked to advise the government on where in the UK economy there are skilled labour shortages that can be 'sensibly' addressed by immigration from outside the European Economic Area (EEA). 'Skilled', 'shortage', and 'sensible' are all defined and operationalized by the MAC. A recent proposal for immigration reform in the US, supported by the two major trades unions, includes the establishment of an independent Foreign Workers Adjustment Commission to "measure labour shortages and recommend the numbers and characteristics of employment-based temporary and permanent immigrants to fill those shortages" (Marshall 2009).

All these policy initiatives, and any efforts to link labour immigration to domestic labour shortages more generally, need to address the same fundamental questions: how do we define, measure, and assess various policy responses to staff shortages? Put differently, in terms of the specific policy question, how should the Government evaluate and respond to employers' claims that migrants are "needed to fill labour and skills shortages" and "to do the jobs that domestic workers cannot or will not do"? This chapter reviews some of the key issues and insights from existing research for addressing these key questions that are at the heart of labour immigration policy in all countries.

4.2 SHORTAGES AND SKILLS ARE SLIPPERY CONCEPTS THAT ARE DIFFICULT TO DEFINE AND MEASURE

Both shortages and skills are highly slippery concepts. There is no universally accepted definition of a labour or skills shortage and no one obvious 'optimal' policy response. The definition of shortage typically underlying employers' calls for migrants to help fill vacancies is that the demand for labour exceeds supply at the prevailing wages and employment conditions. Most media reports of 'labour and skills shortages' are based on surveys that ask employers about hard-to-fill jobs at current wages and employment conditions.

In contrast, a basic economic approach emphasises the role of the price mechanism in bringing markets that are characterised by excess demand or excess supply into equilibrium. In a simple textbook model of a competitive labour market, where demand and supply of labour are critically determined by the price of labour, most shortages are temporary and eventually eliminated by rising wages that increase supply and reduce demand. Of course, in practice, labour markets do not always work as the simple textbook model suggests. Prices can be 'sticky', and whether and how quickly prices clear labour markets critically depend on the reasons for labour shortages, which can include sudden increases in demand and/or inflexible supply. Nevertheless, the fundamental point of the economic approach remains that the existence and size of shortages critically depend on the price of labour (MAC 2008).

Similarly, although commonly used in academic, public, and policy discourse, 'skills' is a very vague term both conceptually and empirically. It can refer to a wide range of qualifications and competencies whose meaning in practice is not always clear. Some 'skills' are credentialised (e.g. National Vocational Qualifications, professional qualifications, and apprenticeships), but what is and is not credentialised changes and jobs can shift from being classified as 'low-skilled' to 'skilled' and vice versa without necessarily changing in their content. The limitation of formal qualifications as a measure of skills becomes most apparent when one considers 'soft' skills not captured through formal qualifications. They cover a broad range of competencies, transferable across occupations (rather than being specialised) from 'problem solving' to 'teamworking' and 'customer-handling skills'. Soft skills are often said to be particularly important in sectors where social relations with customers, clients, and/or service users are important to the delivery and quality of the work. Certain 'skills' may be necessary to make sure the job is done in a way that contributes to a good service experience, rather than simply to complete the task. For example, the quality of care delivered in both health and social care sectors is affected by the soft skills of those providing care, with some service users actively expressing a preference for personal qualities over formal qualifications.

At the same time, 'skills' can also be used to refer to attributes and characteristics that are related to employer control over the workforce. A demand for soft skills can easily shade into a demand for employees with specific personal characteristics and behaviour (Payne 2000). Employers may find certain qualities and attitudes desirable because they suggest workers will be compliant, easy to discipline, and cooperative. The fuzziness of 'skill' is further exacerbated by its application to demeanour, accent, style, and even physical appearance (Warhurst and Nickson 2007). As skills soften, these signifiers may assume greater importance for those occupations which are less strictly regulated regarding formal qualifications and where employers consequently have greater discretion in recruitment.

Any discussion of 'skills shortages' needs to be aware that employers play an important role in defining the competencies and attributes that are 'needed' to do particular jobs and in deciding the terms and conditions of the job. In some occupations, the skills and 'work ethic' demanded by employers are partly or largely a reflection of employer preference for a workforce over which they can exercise particular mechanisms of control and/or that is prepared to accept wages and employment conditions that do not attract a sufficient supply of domestic workers.

4.3   WHY SOME EMPLOYERS PREFER MIGRANT WORKERS

A key consideration in assessment of employer demand for migrant workers is that 'what employers want' (i.e. the skills, competencies and attributes required of employees) is critically influenced by what employers 'think they can get' from the available pools of labour (Ruhs and Anderson 2010). The labour supply potentially available to employers (e.g. the unemployed, inactive, migrant workers, etc.) is highly diverse, has different expectations and is differently motivated to participate in the labour market. It is easy to see how, faced with a diverse pool of labour, employers can become increasingly 'picky' and demanding of the types of workers they 'need'. This raises the possibility that employers develop a preference for migrant workers (or particular types of migrant workers) over domestic workers based on migrants' perceived superior characteristics and attributes (Waldinger and Lichter 2003). This is in practice reflected in employers' common claims that migrants have superior 'work ethic' and 'attitude'. These sorts of claims are typically made for relatively new arrivals rather than for foreign-born individuals more generally. A number of factors may encourage employers to develop such a preference.

Some employers may prefer migrants because of their lower expectations about wages and employment conditions. Research suggests that employers are typically acutely aware of the economic and other trade-offs that new migrants are willing to make by tolerating wages and employment conditions that are poor by the standards of their host country but higher than those prevailing in their countries of origin, and this is not confined to the lowest-paying occupations and sectors in the labour market (Anderson et al. 2006). In the UK, some employers in some sectors such as agriculture openly acknowledge that the wages and employment conditions they offer for low-skilled work are considered unacceptable to most British workers.

Second, some employers in EU countries may develop a preference for migrants from outside of the EU because of the characteristics and restrictions attached to their immigration status (see e.g. Bloomekatz 2007). In most high-income countries, immigration policies are characterised by a multitude of different types of status. Each status (such as work- permit holder, student, working holidaymaker, and dependent) is associated with different rights and restrictions in and beyond the labour market. Certain types of restrictions, such as the requirement to work for the employer specified on the work permit only, may give rise to a specific demand for particular types of migrant workers. Some employers, especially those finding it difficult to retain workers in certain jobs, may prefer workers whose choice of employment is restricted within the host country, as is usually the case with recent arrivals and migrants on temporary visas. Immigration requirements can make it difficult for migrants to change jobs. From the employer's perspective, the employment restrictions associated with particular types of immigration status may make migrants more 'suitable' and easier to retain in jobs that offer low wages and poor employment conditions (Anderson 2010).

Third, because of their different frame of reference, new migrants may be prepared to accept jobs whose skill requirements are significantly below their actual skills and qualifications, creating "high quality workers for low-waged jobs", who may well be more attractive employees than the available domestic workforce. In some cases, employer demand for particular groups of migrant labour may reflect a demand for specified skills or knowledge related to particular countries, including foreign language skills. In a globalised economy, in both high and low-skilled sectors, employers may value the knowledge and contacts migrants bring from their countries of origin. Whether or not these specialised skills which are related to particular countries or regions can be taught to, and acquired by, local workers, and consequently, whether certain products, trade links, and services can only be provided by workers from particular countries is more contested in low- and medium-skilled occupations such as mid-level chefs in ethnic cuisine restaurants than in high-skilled occupations such as financial services.

The perceived advantages of recruiting migrants can also include employers' preference for a 'self-regulating' and 'self-sustaining' labour supply (Rodriguez 2004). Employers can use migrant networks to control and regulate the flow of labour. Recruitment through migrant networks is thought to be a very common practice among employers with a migrant workforce. Companies with a demand for a flexible workforce may make use of employment agencies to help find suitable workers. Since employment agencies often have significant numbers of migrant workers on their books, they can play an important role in impacting on the national composition of the workforce.

4.4   ALTERNATIVES TO IMMIGRATION

In theory, at an individual level, employers may respond to perceived staff shortages in different ways. These include: (i) increasing wages and/or improving working conditions to attract more citizens who are either inactive, unemployed, or employed in other sectors, and/or to increase the working hours of the existing workforce; this may require a change in recruitment processes and greater investment in training and up- skilling; (ii) changing the production process to make it less labour intensive by, for example, increasing the capital and/or technology intensity; (iii) relocating to countries where labour costs are lower; (iv) switching to production (provision) of less labour-intensive commodities and services; and (v) employing migrant workers.

Of course, not all of these options will be available to all employers at all times. For example, most construction, health, social care and hospitality work cannot be off-shored. An employer's decision on how to respond to a perceived labour shortage will naturally depend in part on the relative cost of each of the feasible alternatives. If there is ready access to cheap migrant labour, employers may not consider the alternatives to immigration as a way of reducing staff shortages. This may be in the short-term interest of employers but perhaps not in the best interest of the sector or the national economy. There is clearly the danger that the recruitment of migrants to fill perceived labour and skills needs in the short run exacerbates shortages and thus entrenches the certain low-cost and migrant-intensive production systems in the long run.

System Effects
It is important to recognise that employers do not make their choices in a vacu-

um. Employers' recruitment decisions are in many ways constrained by 'system effects' that include the wider institutional and regulatory framework that is, to a large degree, created by public policies. Public policies often incentivise employers in some sectors and occupations to respond to shortages through the employment of migrant workers – and in some cases leave them little choice. For example, the UK has long prided itself on its labour market flexibility and its relatively low levels of labour regulation. Together with a range of policies from training to housing, this stance has contributed to creating a growing demand for migrant workers.

In the construction sector, for example, the difficulty of finding suitably skilled British workers is critically related to low levels of labour market regulation and the absence of a comprehensive vocational education and training system (for more detailed discussion see Chan, Clarke and Dainty 2010). The industry is highly fragmented. It relies on temporary, project-based labour, informal recruitment and casualised employment. These practices may have proved profitable in the short term, but they have eroded employers' incentive to invest in long-term training. As a consequence, vocational education provisions are inadequate for the sector. By contrast, many other European states, such as Germany and Poland, have well-developed training and apprenticeship programmes, producing workers with a wide range of transferable skills. It is often some of these workers (especially Polish workers since May 2004) who have been doing jobs in Britain such as groundwork, or foundation-building, which is low-paid and which has no formal training requirement, despite years of lobbying by contractors.

Social care is another sector in the UK where public policies have created an increasing demand for migrant workers (Moriarty 2010; Cangiano et al. 2009). Two thirds of care assistants in London are migrants. The shortages of social-care workers and care assistants are largely due to low wages and poor working conditions. Most social care in the UK is publicly funded, but actually provided by the private sector and voluntary organisations. Constraints in local authority budgets have contributed to chronic underinvestment. Together with the structure of the care sector itself, this approach has resulted in a growing demand for low-wage, flexible workers. Simply cutting benefits, or reducing legal access to migrant workers without addressing the causes of British workers' reluctance to apply for jobs in the sector, will put more pressure on an already creaking system.

Path Dependence in the Employment of Migrants
There can be 'path dependencies' in the employment of migrants in the sense that once their workforce includes a substantial share of migrants it may be difficult and costly for employers to switch to alternative responses. In other

words, immigration targeted to address short-term shortages may help sustain the conditions (such as relatively low wages, poor working conditions, little training of domestic workers, low propensities for employers to adopt new technologies and, importantly, low status) that encourage shortages of domestic workers in the long run. There is a supply-side element to path dependence: it can combine with migratory patterns driven by cumulative causation to ensure a ready supply of new arrivals – through family reunion if not through labour market programmes (Massey 1990; Dobson et al. 2009). Moreover, in the same way that jobs done by men can become 'women's jobs' (Goldin 1994: 302), jobs previously done by (white) citizens can become 'migrant jobs' and therefore lower status. The converse, however, is much more difficult and it is not easy for jobs to regain social status once they have been performed by stigmatised groups, even if pay and conditions improve (Gordon and Lenhardt 2008: 301).

These processes can lead to what Cornelius and others have called a 'structural embeddedness' of the demand for migrant workers in the economy (Cornelius 1998). This 'structural embeddedness' is a consequence of the long-standing and mutually constitutive nature of supply and demand. It can also be related to wider labour market developments such as: labour market segmentations, where specific types of workers are matched and become associated with particular types of jobs; economic restructuring (Champlin and Hake 2006, Johnston 2007); and the emergence of 'dead-end' jobs and a 'low-skills equilibrium', where "a self-reinforcing network of societal and state institutions....interact to stifle the demand for improvements in skill levels" (Finegold and Sosicke 1988: 22; also see Keep and Mayhew 1999, Payne 2000).

4.5   MIND THE GAP: LABOUR IMMIGRATION AND PUBLIC POLICY

Linking the admission of new migrant workers to labour and skills shortages requires critical analyses of what constitutes 'skills' and 'shortages', how to measure them, and debate about whether immigration is the best response to the shortage. While the first two questions are challenging, it is important to recognise that the third question about alternative responses to shortages is an inherently normative issue that does not have a single 'right' answer. Deciding whether the optimal response to shortages should be additional migrants, higher wages, or some other option is a necessarily political issue that requires a balancing of competing interests.

Immigration is often viewed as a discrete area of policy, and the relationships between immigration, labour demand and other policy areas typically remain unexplored in public debates. An important insight of this chapter is that the

increasing reliance on migrant workers in many sectors is not – as it is sometimes argued – simply a consequence of 'lax immigration controls'. Neither can
it be reduced to slogans such as 'exploitative employers', "lazy locals won't do
the work", or "migrants are needed for economic recovery". The increasing
demand for migrant workers in high-income countries often arises from a
broad range of institutions, public policies and social relations. Reducing or at
least slowing down the growth in this reliance – which is a policy goal of many
Governments – will not happen without fundamental changes to the policies
and institutions that create the demand. The specific public policy changes required will vary across countries. In the UK they include greater labour market
regulation in some sectors, more investment in education and training, better
wages and conditions in some low-wage public sector jobs, improved job status
and career tracks, better regulation of recruitment agencies and a decline in low-
wage agency work. In the short- to medium-term, some of these changes are
unlikely because of the economic downturn and budget cuts, which may well
in fact increase demand for migrants in low-wage sectors.

Whatever the policy goal in terms of regulating the scale of immigration, the
key conclusion of this chapter is that any debate about labour immigration
policy needs to carefully consider the links between immigration and a wide
range of public policies, and discuss the demand for migrant workers in the
context of the host country's 'economic and social model' as a whole. Ignoring
these links runs the risk of ignoring important drivers of labour immigration,
thus undermining the effectiveness of any policies that regulate the admission
of migrant workers.

NOTES

1   This article is based on the analysis in M. Ruhs and B. Anderson (eds.) (2010) *Who Needs Migrant Workers? Labour Shortages, Immigration and Public Policy*, Oxford University Press (paperback published in 2012).

REFERENCES

Anderson, B. (2010) 'Migration, Immigration Controls and the Fashioning of Precarious Workers', *Work, Employment and Society* 24, 2: 300-317.

Anderson, B., M. Ruhs, S. Spencer and B. Rogaly (2006) *'Fair Enough? Central and East European Low Wage Migrants in Low Wage Employment in the UK'*, Report written for the Joseph Rowntree Foundation, Centre on Policy, Migration and Society, Oxford: University of Oxford.

Bloomekatz, R. (2007) 'Rethinking Immigration Status Discrimination and Exploitation in the Low-Wage Workplace', *UCLA Law Review* 54, 6: 1963– 2010.

Cangiano, A., I. Shutes, S. Spencer and G. Leeson (2009) 'Migrant Care Workers in Ageing Societies: Research Findings in the United Kingdom', *Centre on Migration, Policy and Society*, Oxford: University of Oxford.

Champlin, D. and E. Hake (2006) 'Immigration as Industrial strategy in American Meatpacking', *Review of Political Economy* 18, 1: 49-69.

Chan, P., L. Clarke and A. Dainty (2010) 'The Dynamics of Migrant Employment in Construction: Can Supply of Skilled Labour ever Match Demand?', Chap. 7 in Martin Ruhs and Bridget Anderson (eds.) *Who Needs Migrant Workers? Labour Shortages, Immigration and Public Policy*, Oxford: Oxford University Press.

Cornelius, W. (1998) 'The Structural Embeddedness of Demand for Mexican Immigrant Labour: New Evidence from California' in M. Suarez-Orozco (ed.) *Crossings: Mexican Immigration in Interdisciplinary Perspective*, Cambridge M.A.

Dobson, J., A. Latham J. and Salt (2009) *On the Move? Labour Migration in Times of Recession. What Can We Learn from the Past?*, London: Policy Network.

Financial Times (2009) 'FT poll reveals hostility to jobless migrants', March 15.

Finch, T., M. Latorre, N. Pollard and J. Rutter (2009) *'Shall We Stay or Shall We Go? Re-migration Trends among Britain's Immigrants'*, London: Institute for Public Policy Research.

Finegold, D. and D. Sosicke (1988) 'The Failure of Training in Britain: Analysis and Prescription', *Oxford Review of Economic Policy* 4, 3: 1-15.

Goldin, C. (1994) 'Understanding the Gender Gap: an Economic History of American Women' in P. Burstein (ed.) *Equal Employment Opportunity: Labor Market Discrimination and Public Policy*, Chicago: University of Chicago Press.

Gordon, J. and R. Lenhardt (2008) 'Rethinking Work and Citizenship', *UCLA Law Review* 55: 1161-1238.

Johnston, D. (2007) 'Who Needs Immigrant Farm Workers? A South African Case Study', *Journal of Agrarian Change* 7, 4: 406-421.

Keep, E. and K. Mayhew (1999) 'The Assessment: Knowledge, Skills and Competitiveness', *Oxford Review of Economic Policy* 15, 1: 1-15.

Lucas, R. (1988) 'On the Mechanics of Economic Development', *Journal of Monetary Economics* 22, 1: 3–42.

Marshall, R. (2009) *Immigration for Shared Prosperity - A Framework for Comprehen-*

sive Reform, Washington: Economic Policy Institute (EPI).

Massey, D. (1990) 'Social Structure, Household Strategies and the Cumulative Causation of Migration', *Population Index* 65, 1: 3-26.

Migration Advisory Committee (MAC) (2008) *'Skilled, Shortage and Sensible, The First Shortage Occupation List for the uk and Scotland'*, London: Home Office.

Migration Advisory Committee (2010) *'Limits on Migration'*, London: Home Office.

Moriarty, J. (2010) 'Competing with Myths: Migrant Labour in Social Care', Chap. 5 in Martin Ruhs and Bridget Anderson (eds.) *Who Needs Migrant Workers? Labour Shortages, Immigration and Public Policy*, Oxford: Oxford University Press.

Payne, J. (2000) 'The Unbearable Lightness of Skill: The Changing Meaning of Skill in UK Policy Discourses and Some Implications for Education and Training', *Journal of Education Policy* 15, 3: 353–69.

Rodriguez, N. (2004) 'Workers Wanted': Employer Recruitment of Immigrant Labour', *Work and Occupations* 31, 4: 453-73.

Romer, P. (1986) 'Increasing Returns and Long-Run Growth', *Journal of Political Economy*, 94: 1002-37.

Ruhs, M. and B. Anderson, (eds.) (hardback 2010, paperback 2012) *Who Needs Migrant Workers? Labour Shortages, Immigration and Public Policy*, Oxford: Oxford University Press.

Waldinger, R.D. and M. Lichter (2003) *How the Other Half Works: Immigration and the Social Organization of Labor*, Berkeley: University of California Press.

Warhurst, C. and D. Nickson (2007) 'A New Labour Aristocracy? Aesthetic Labour and Routine Interactive Service', *Work, Employment and Society* 21, 4: 785-98.

5 INTRA-EU LABOUR MOBILITY AFTER EASTERN ENLARGEMENT AND DURING THE CRISIS: MAIN TRENDS AND CONTROVERSIES[1]

Béla Galgóczi and Janine Leschke

5.1 INTRODUCTION

The accession of eight new Central and Eastern European countries (EU8)[2] to the EU in May 2004 and the subsequent accession of Romania and Bulgaria in January 2007 (EU2) marked an important step in the history of European integration. It reunited a continent divided since the Second World War. An important consequence was the extension of the free movement of capital, goods, services and people to Central and Eastern Europe. European law guarantees these freedoms within the EU – in principle. However, in light of the large differences in wages, for example, there were fears of a massive influx of workers from the new Member States with expected negative impacts on the receiving countries' labour markets (and welfare systems). As a result, all but three countries (the United Kingdom, Ireland and Sweden) made use of so-called transitional measures in 2004. These transitional measures restricted – to varying degrees – the right to work for EU8 citizens in EU15 countries for a period of up to seven years.

EU15 countries successively opened their labour markets over the subsequent years, however, and only Germany and Austria made use of the entire seven-year transition period, fully opening up their labour markets only in May 2011. Workers from Bulgaria and Romania will not have complete freedom of movement until January 2014; currently, 11 Member States still have transitional measures in place with regard to EU2 workers, in several cases with simplified procedures or exceptions for certain groups of workers or certain sectors.[3] The darkening economic outlook from the summer of 2007 onwards was a major factor here. Interestingly, Spain temporarily re-introduced restrictions on new Romanian workers in July 2011, a step that was justified with reference to the labour market impact of the crisis.[4]

Post-2004 labour mobility constitutes a historically new phenomenon in a number of respects, exhibiting characteristics that distinguish it from its previous forms as a result of EU enlargements. First of all, it is a multifaceted process, with different forms of labour mobility co-existing in a rapidly changing environment, a factor whose importance has more recently been further accentuated by the economic crisis. Different forms of cross-border labour mobility include commuting, short-term, circular and more permanent migration, but functional equivalents of migration as (bogus) self- employment and posted work also play an important role. It is also new that migrants from low-wage countries have a comparably high educational profile in absolute terms and in relation to nationals in the target countries.

The examples of the UK and Ireland, which experienced large inflows of migrant workers upon enlargement, illustrate that historical migration patterns and pre-enlargement labour flows were redirected geographically towards those EU15 countries that opened up their labour markets right after enlargement while simultaneously displaying favourable conditions in terms of labour market demand (see also Holland et al. 2011).[5] This shift can also be shown for the largest EU8 country, Poland. In the period 1999-2003, Germany had been the major destination country for labour migration from Poland. After EU enlargement, the UK became the principal destination country. Indeed, the share of the three countries that did not maintain labour market restrictions after enlargement grew from 12.1 per cent to 42.4 per cent of Polish migrants (Fihel and Okólski 2009). The presence of transitional measures thus seems to have had a diversion effect on quantitative migration flows. However, the interaction of these measures with other push and pull factors, in particular labour demand (employment opportunities), but also language, cultural proximity and migrant networks, is complex.

This article addresses a range of questions in an attempt to characterise the trends in intra-EU cross-border labour mobility of recent years. In the first section, we use data from the European Labour Force Survey (see annex for details) to show European trends in cross-border labour mobility during the crisis, also taking account of the labour market outcomes for migrant and local workers. In a further step, we address migration under the services directive, particularly the phenomenon of bogus self-employment. The argument is often made that migrant workers can compensate for skills needs in the receiving labour markets, but there has been little study of the extent to which migrant workers are able to use their specific skills in receiving labour markets. In this article we cite some evidence from the largest recipient countries of EU10 migration, Italy and the UK. Finally, we assess a number of the policy responses of receiving countries to post-enlargement intra-EU migration.

5.2   THE MAIN TRENDS OF POST-ENLARGEMENT INTRA-EU LABOUR MOBILITY WITH SPECIAL ATTENTION TO THE PERIOD OF THE CRISIS[6]

Figure 5.1 illustrates that the broad developments of East-West labour mobility since enlargement in 2004 and up to the crisis show a marked increase in the EU8 migrant population in the two receiving countries (United Kingdom and Ireland) that opened their labour market from the beginning and at the same time had comparatively favourable labour market situations at that time.[7] The negative impact of the crisis on post-2008 labour migration from Central and Eastern European countries, however, is visible in both countries and particularly in Ireland, which was hard hit by the crisis.

At the same time, Germany – a traditional destination country for CEE migrants but which maintained restrictions until May 2011 – still shows steady but moderate growth in its EU8 population without any visible effect of the crisis (Figure 5.1). In light of the recent positive labour market developments in Germany (Leschke and Watt 2010), in contrast to most other EU15 countries, one might have even expected a more pronounced positive trend in the past two years than that observed.

Against this background, it is important to note that due to continuing EU10 migration inflow, the overall stock of EU10 population in EU15 countries has continued to grow during the crisis (except in Ireland and Spain).[8] This occurred in the face of declining overall employment (except in Germany and Poland) and seemingly contradicts previous expectations in the literature that deep recessions result in a setback in migration flows and concrete forecasts that this would happen in the European post-crisis context.

Figure 5.1   EU8 population in major EU15 receiving countries, 2005-2011 ('000; stocks)

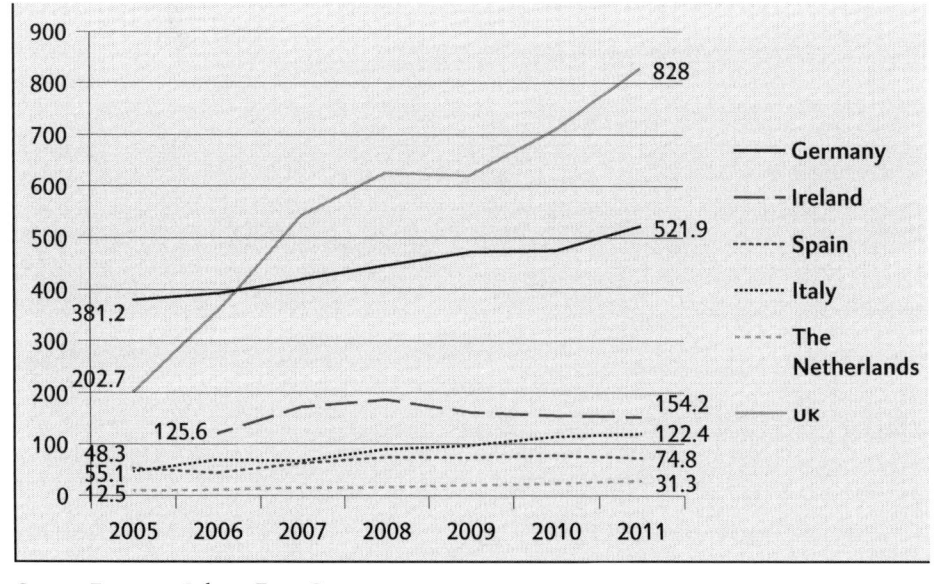

Source: European Labour Force Survey.

Within this overall trend, however, migration from EU8 and EU2 countries showed different dynamics during the crisis, which can be explained by the fact that not only receiving countries but also sending countries differed markedly with regard to the labour market impacts of the crisis, which had a key role in shaping migration push factors. Poland, the country with by far the largest migration flows in absolute terms, has done comparatively well during the crisis (push factors were thus less intensive), whereas the Baltic countries in particular experienced huge increases in unemployment and declines in employment, particularly in the initial phase of the crisis (push factors intensified). Indeed during the crisis we observe temporary reductions in EU8 and, more particularly, Polish migrants (with signs of return migration) (Fihel and Anacka 2012) but a growing intensity of labour flows from Bulgaria and Romania (EU2), particularly to Italy, as Figure 5.2 shows. The increase in EU2 flows should also be seen in light of the later accession of these countries and the enormous economic (e.g. wages) and social differences between them and the EU15 countries.

Changes in receiving country composition were also observed, as receiving countries hard hit by the crisis (Spain and Ireland) saw a net decrease in EU10 migration stock, while all other receiving countries experienced further growth (especially Italy) (Figure 5.3). Two factors were decisive for the size of EU10 migration stock in the EU15 receiving countries, as well as its changes during

Figure 5.2   EU2 population in receiving countries, 2005-2011 ('000; stocks)

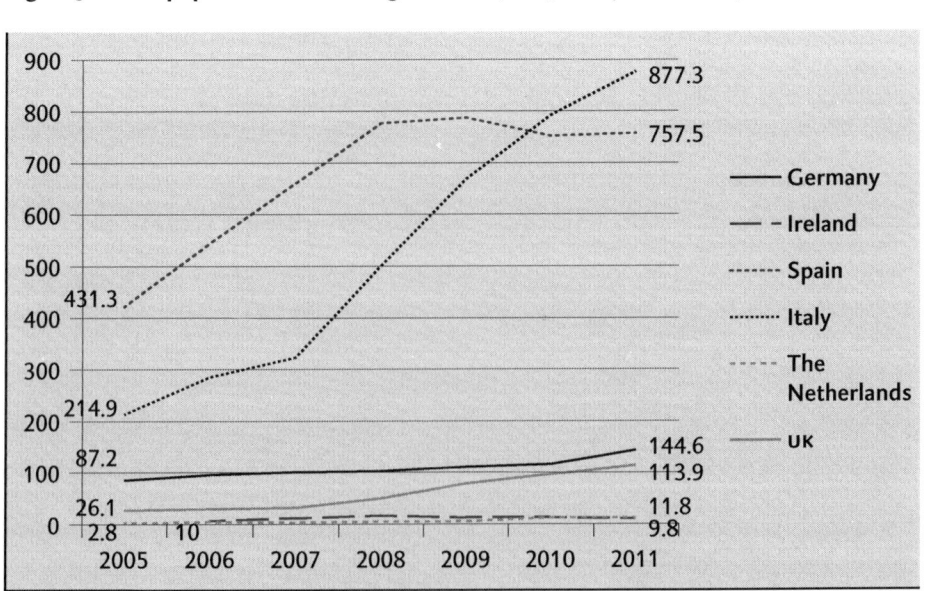

Source: European Labour Force Survey.

the crisis: labour market access and the extent to which a receiving country was hit by the crisis (labour demand).

When looking at smaller EU15 economies, we see considerable differentiation in the extent to which their labour markets absorbed EU10 migrants. The Netherlands had a very favourable labour market situation at the time of the 2004 accession, with one of the lowest unemployment rates in Europe, and it was also not particularly hard hit by the crisis. Moreover, it lifted transitional measures for EU8 citizens relatively early. Even if both EU8 and EU2 migration stocks in the Netherlands doubled between 2008 and 2011 to 31,300 and 9800 respectively, it only received a fraction of the EU8 and EU2 migrants that went to smaller countries such as Ireland, Austria, Greece and Belgium (see Figure 5.3). The greater attractiveness of both Austria and Greece can be explained at least in part by their geographic proximity to the accession countries, and Ireland surely profited from opening its labour market immediately upon accession and from language advantages. It is, however, hard to find any plausible explanation as to why the Netherlands was so little affected when, at the same time, another Benelux country, Belgium, with much less favourable labour market conditions and longer application of transitional measures (until May 2009 as compared to January 2007), saw much larger growth during the initial

Figure 5.3: **Impact of the crisis on stocks of EU10 nationals in EU15 countries, working-age population ('000)**

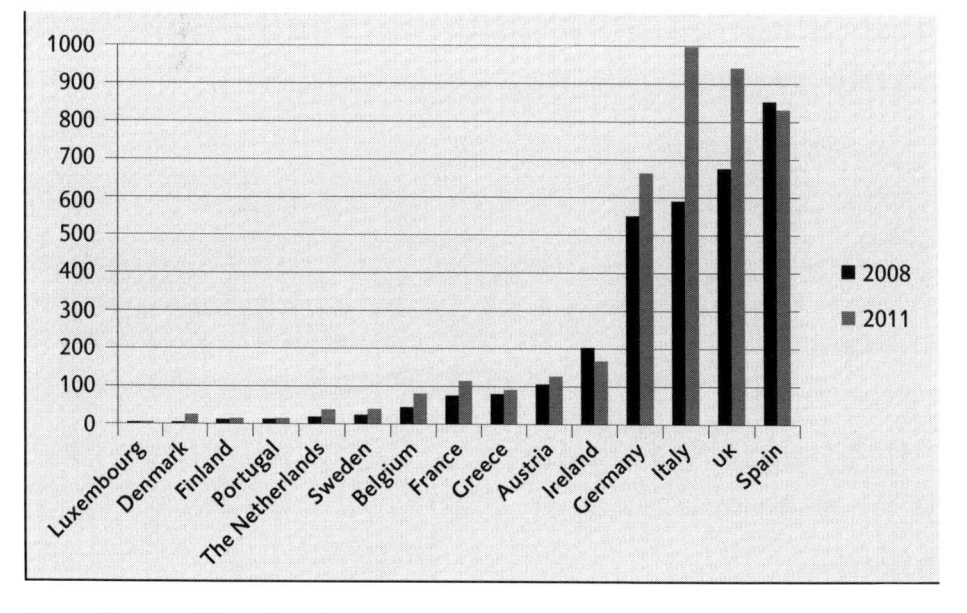

Source: European Labour Force Survey.

crisis period and had about triple the stock of EU10 migrant workers in 2011
(Figure 5.3).[9] Even considering the upward trend over the whole accession
period, the Netherlands appears to be an outlier with regard to EU10 inflows;
the question remains why it proved to be relatively unattractive to regular EU10
migrant workers.

As regards the direct impact of the crisis on labour market outcomes, EU10
migrants were harder hit in the majority of EU15 countries and at least partially
acted as labour market buffers. This can be illustrated by looking at recent
changes in employment rates for nationals and EU10 migrants (Figure 5.4).
Both groups saw declines in employment rates in the majority of EU15 countries, but the trend was stronger for EU10 migrants; they were, for example,
considerably more affected by declining employment in Denmark, Ireland
and Portugal. At the same time, unemployment increased and EU10 migrants
were again disproportionately affected (not shown here). In principle EU
migrant workers have the same rights to unemployment benefits as nationals;
in practice, however, they are often covered to a lesser extent because they are
not only less aware of their rights but are also more often in irregular and non-
standard forms of employment with no or reduced eligibility for unemployment benefits. The greater vulnerability of EU10 workers in the crisis reflects
to a considerable extent the higher concentration of such workers in sectors
disproportionately affected by the slump in output; job losses were, for example, extremely heavy in construction, which shed more than four and a quarter
million jobs in the EU15 and employs a high concentration of EU10 workers.

**Figure 5.4   Employment rate of nationals and of EU10 citizens before and after the crisis
(in %)**

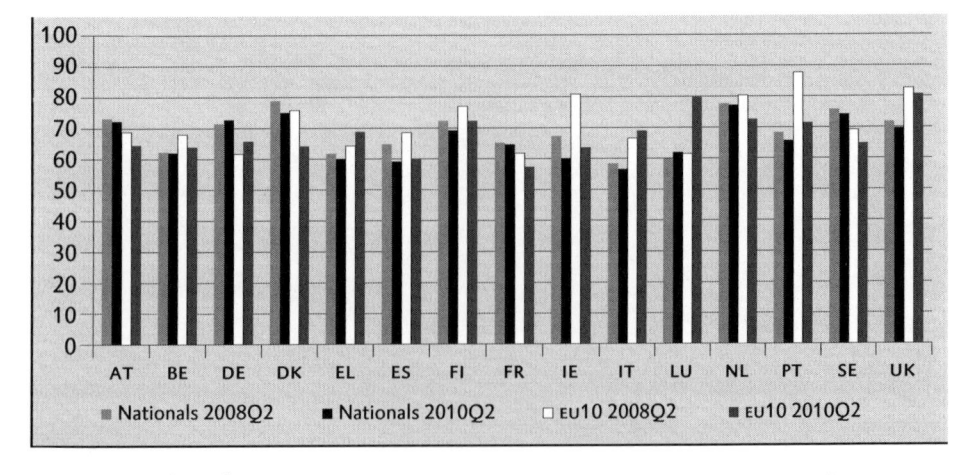

Source: European Labour Force Survey.

The trends described above suggest that both push and pull factors were subject to dynamic changes in this turbulent period. For some sending countries, such as Romania and Latvia, push factors (effects of the crisis on local labour markets, insufficient welfare system, etc.) remained the dominant force of labour migration during the crisis. Migrant workers from other sending countries were faced with the emergence of return options, a case in point being Poland with a comparably good labour demand situation during the crisis. Complex combinations of both push and pull factors were also observed with onwards migration from formerly very attractive receiving countries hard hit by the crisis, such as Ireland, to destinations with better labour market prospects.

To conclude, migration flows and trends upon accession and during the crisis were impacted by:
- Labour market demand and the characteristics of jobs taken by migrant workers in the receiving country, including the impact of the crisis on the labour market as a whole (e.g. rising unemployment, declining employment) and on particular sectors such as construction and manufacturing, which were popular among migrant workers;
- The impact of the economic crisis on the labour market situation as well as the extent to which unemployment benefits were available in the source country (as potential push factors);
- The additional accession of two new Member States in 2007, with Bulgarian and Romanian workers being permitted to work legally in EU15 countries, although with temporary restrictions in the majority of these countries under the transitional measures;
- Changing migration policy in receiving countries throughout the period, with full versus gradual opening of labour markets due to the differences in their application of the transitional measures.

5.3   LABOUR MOBILITY UNDER THE SERVICES DIRECTIVE

One of the most controversial issues in the EU labour mobility debate, not least in the context of transitional measures imposed by most Member States, has been the possible substitution of regular employment by functional equivalents such as posted work or (bogus) self-employment, making use of and in some cases abusing the freedom of service provision in order to circumvent restrictions imposed as transitional measures on waged employment.[10] The decisions by the European Court of Justice in the Viking and Laval cases, which challenged a number of social rights (e.g. the right to collective bargaining and the right to strike), exemplify the complex situation concerning the posting of workers under the freedom of services (Brücker and Warneck 2010). A European Directive on Posting of Workers had already been put in place in 1996. In

Figure 5.5   Self-employed (without employees) as share of total employment, by nationality, 2008Q1 and 2011Q1

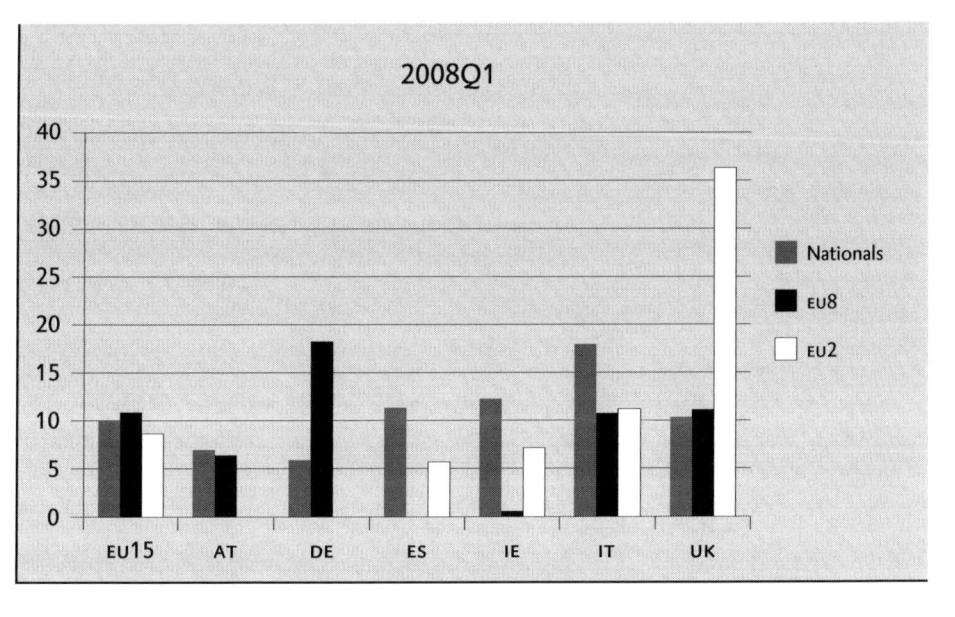

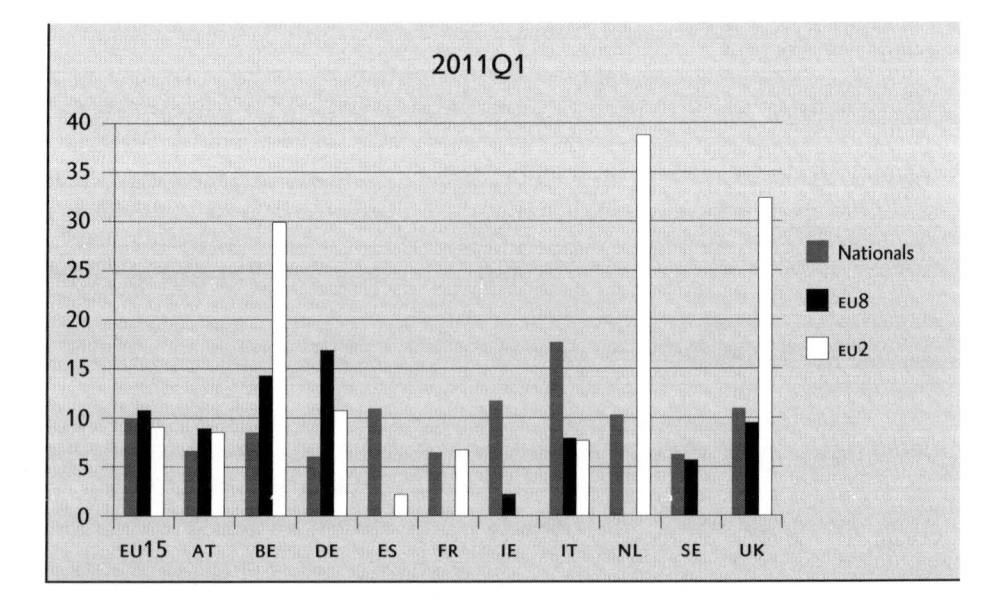

Notes: Some columns are not shown due to missing values (small case numbers); in cases where no information on EU8 or EU2 was available, the country has been dropped from the panel (BE, NL, FR for 2008Q1).
Source: European Labour Force Survey, special data extraction.

response to the post-2004 labour mobility challenges and the case law mentioned above, which stirred ardent public debate, in March 2012 the European Commission proposed both an enforcement directive, meant to improve the way the 1996 directive is implemented in practice – in particular with regard to the rights of workers – and a new regulation aiming to clarify the relationship between the right to take collective action and the freedom of services (see also Cremers 2011). These proposals[11] are currently being discussed at EU level.

There are no reliable comparative figures available on the number of posted workers. Special extraction of LFS data allows us to break total employment down into employees, family workers, self-employed persons with employees of their own, and those without. We are primarily interested in the split between employees and the self-employed without employees of their own, as this gives us an idea of the importance of (bogus) self-employment among migrant workers as opposed to dependent employment.[12]

As the share of self-employment (without employees) is roughly the same for all three groups (nationals, EU2 and EU8 migrants) at the aggregate EU15 level, we see little evidence of widespread (ab)use of the status of self-employment (at least provided there is not substantial underreporting of self-employed vis-à-vis employed migrants) (Figure 5.5).[13]

However, the national figures show a highly differentiated picture. A case in point is Germany, where the rate of self-employment (without employees) is around 18 per cent for EU8 and 10 per cent for EU2 (2011 figures only), compared to around 6 per cent for natives. This is highly suggestive of the use of self-employment as a means of avoiding the transitional measures imposed by that country. A similar overall pattern emerges in the Netherlands and Belgium, with own-account self-employment among EU2 migrants being up to four times higher than among nationals.[14] Both countries still have transitional measures in place for EU2 workers with some simplifications.[15] The United Kingdom is also very illustrative. The proportion of self-employed among EU8 migrant workers – to whom no transitional measures applied – is broadly in line with the figure for natives (at a fairly high level of around 10 per cent). But among EU2 workers, who remain subject to such measures, the level of self-employment is more than three times as high.

The picture is reversed in the southern EU15 countries for which we have robust data (and for Ireland). Here, a high proportion of native workers is self-employed (many of them in agriculture), whereas the self-employed share among migrants is typically very low. We have to emphasise here that the data are not likely to pick up short-term seasonal workers and are definitely not picking up illegal migrant work, which is also a phenomenon of EU10 migrant work in agriculture, at least to some extent.

Finally, it should be noted that there are no systematic changes in the shares of own-account self-employment between 2008 and 2011, rising in some countries while falling in others for one or both sub-groups. The crisis does not appear to have had a consistent effect on the split between employees and own account self-employed workers.

We thus do not see 'excessive' recourse to (bogus) self-employment; it is clearly an adjustment strategy used in those countries and by those groups whose access to the labour market is prevented or restricted by the transitional measures.

5.4   SOME EVIDENCE OF A SKILLS/OCCUPATION MISMATCH

Another controversial debate concerns the balance of skills levels of the migrants that different EU countries have managed to attract to their labour markets. Eurostat LFS data enable us to distinguish between three broad skill/education categories: low, medium and high.

The skills composition of EU8 migrants shows significant differences in various receiving countries; this is also true for nationals. Without showing detailed data here, two important features can be identified from the overview of qualification characteristics of EU10 migrant workers in EU15 receiving countries, according to the LFS data. Before the crisis, EU10 workers on EU15 aggregate level were considerably overrepresented in the medium-skilled category (58% compared with 45% for natives) and correspondingly underrepresented, to approximately equal extents, among the low- and high-skilled categories. During the crisis – and again at EU15 aggregate level – their distribution became more balanced, with the share of medium-skilled EU10 migrants decreasing as the shares of both high- and low-skilled migrants rose.

Behind the general trend, changes in two receiving countries are particularly interesting: Italy and the UK. In 2008, the UK had a particularly large share of medium-skilled EU8 migrants. By 2011, however, the situation had changed dramatically and both the share of low- and high-skilled EU8 migrants increased. In Italy, medium-skilled EU10 migrants were also overrepresented, especially the EU2 migrants who make up the bulk of EU10 migration to Italy. What is different in the two receiving countries is that Italy has much smaller shares of high-skilled EU10 migrants than the UK. Moreover, not just EU10 migrants, but also nationals in the UK have a considerably higher skills profile than in Italy. Since the majority of EU8 and EU2 immigrants in Italy have completed

upper secondary education, they are still relatively more educated than both
nationals and non-EU immigrants.

As one of our major interests was the skills/occupation mismatches of EU10
workers in the EU15, we turned our attention to the two receiving countries
that make up a large part of EU10 migration inflow. Bettin, in her contribution to Galgóczi, Leschke and Watt (2012) shows on the basis of more detailed
national LFS data that there is a considerable skills-jobs mismatch among
migrant workers in both the United Kingdom and Italy, with disproportionate
shares of migrant workers in both countries working in blue-collar jobs. While
UK nationals and EU15 citizens are employed mainly in white-collar jobs (56%
and 64% resp. in 2010), the share of blue-collar workers is 82 per cent for EU8
and 79 per cent for EU2 nationals. Over-education thus seems to be far more
widespread across EU8 and EU2 immigrants compared to the other groups. As
regards Italy, while Italian nationals are divided almost evenly between white-
collar and blue-collar jobs, the foreign-born population is fairly polarised. On
the one hand, eight out of ten EU15 citizens work in white-collar jobs, thus
taking advantage of their higher level of human capital. On the other hand, the
remaining groups are concentrated in low-skilled jobs, especially EU2 workers
(who make up the largest share of EU10 migrants by far in Italy).

The extent of over-education among immigrants remained fairly stable in the
UK during the crisis, but this was not the case in Italy. Whereas in 2006 only 20
per cent of EU8 immigrants with tertiary education had low-skilled jobs, their
share increased to close to 50 per cent in 2010. At the same time, the share of
EU2 tertiary educated immigrants employed as blue-collar workers decreased
from a very high 75 per cent in 2006 to 62 per cent by 2010. Thus, the trend
during the crisis went in opposite directions for EU2 and EU8 migrants in Italy,
even though EU2 migrants had been more prone to over-qualification before
the crisis.

Whereas both countries had similar levels of skills-jobs mismatch for migrants
at medium-skill levels, there is less mismatch of high-skilled EU8 and EU2
migrants in Italy than in the UK. Moreover, the skills-jobs match of high-skilled
EU2 migrants in Italy showed improvement during the crisis, although they ac-
counted for a very small share. A change in Italian migration policy with regard
to EU2 citizens might have played a role here, since high-skilled and managerial
jobs were exempted from work permits as far back as early 2007.

The skills picture is rather mixed and it is difficult to draw clear conclusions
from these data. This is not in the least due to the great complexity of the subject, with not only skill levels of both the national and migrant populations
varying from one country to another and over time but also the economic situ-

ation (e.g. crisis) and policies on migrant workers. The following points never-theless seem to be worth noting. When examining the skills characteristics of EU10 migrant workers in the EU15, it is clear that the educational attainment of the EU10 migrant population tends to be significantly higher than in previous migration waves (European Integration Consortium 2009). The issues of 'brain drain', 'brain overflow' and 'brain waste' have been discussed from the point of view of sending countries (for examples, see Kahanec and Zimmermann 2010 and Galgóczi, Leschke and Watt 2009a). One conclusion can certainly be drawn: post-enlargement East-West labour mobility has not contributed to better human-capital allocation due to large-scale skills-occupation mismatch-es affecting EU10 migrants in EU15 labour markets.

5.5   GOVERNMENT AND TRADE UNION POLICIES

The type of measures adopted by governments and the social partners in set-ting and implementing policies related to labour migration vary considerably between individual countries. The first important distinction is, of course, between sending and receiving countries. While governments and the social partners in receiving countries have had to deal with such issues as the integra-tion of the new migrants, protection of their working conditions and wages, and how to maintain the working conditions and wages of indigenous workers, governments and the social partners in sending countries with large emigration flows dealt with a very different set of issues: the most important are linked to rising skills deficits or bottlenecks in certain sectors, which resulted in strate-gies such as the retraining of existing workers, recruitment of migrant workers from neighbouring countries, and initiatives to convince emigrant workers to return home. In this section we focus on policies implemented in receiving countries based on some of the country case studies examined in two books edited by the authors (Galgóczi, Leschke and Watt 2009a, 2012). Information on the policy responses of three of the sending countries (Poland, Latvia and Hungary) can be found in the aforementioned volumes and in Galgóczi, Leschke and Watt (2009b).

With regard to the type of measures adopted in receiving countries, the impo-sition of transitional measures was clearly the most important. Governments in Germany and Austria had to negotiate and implement various exceptions to these measures for certain sectors and occupational groups – mostly high-skill professions or, conversely, areas with unattractive pay and conditions that had trouble recruiting domestic workers – in order to respond to emerging skill deficits and ensure a continued supply of seasonal labour. They also had to re-spond – by way of tighter controls – to an increase in irregular migration (bogus self-employment, posted work, illegal work and the like) which was used to

circumvent the transitional measures and resulted in a loss of social contributions and tax revenues. In both Germany and Austria – in contrast to the UK
and Sweden, for example – trade unions and to some extent also employers'
organisations were in favour of the transitional measures. Trade unions – at
least in Germany – were also eager to influence the migration agenda by lobbying the government on certain issues and laws, instituting some cross-border
cooperation (in both cases sometimes in cooperation with employers) and by
informing migrant workers about their rights. It should be noted that although
both Germany and Austria argued that transitional measures would allow them
to gradually adapt to the free movement of labour, neither of the two countries
has developed a general policy framework with regard to the obligatory lifting
of transitional measures by 2011.[16]

The UK and Sweden – together with Ireland – lifted all restrictions on the free
movement of labour upon the accession of the EU8 countries. Here, the scale
of the migrant inflows played a decisive role in determining the type and extent
of the actions taken by governments and the social partners.[17] In response to the
sheer numbers of migrant workers – which far surpassed that initially predicted
– the UK government, in close consultation with the social partners (not eve-
ryday practice in the UK!), put a number of services for migrant workers into
place but also strengthened the control mechanisms in order to prevent illegal
employment and exploitation of migrant workers. The national trade union
confederations of Ireland and the United Kingdom – the Irish Congress of
Trade Unions (ICTU) and the Trades Union Congress (TUC) respectively –
both supported the principle of free movement of workers from the EU8
Member States. They also objected to the Irish and UK governments' decision
to restrict migrant workers' access to certain welfare benefits. The two union
movements have, however, differed in their stances towards Romanian and
Bulgarian migrant workers. While the TUC opposed the UK government's
decision to restrict EU2 workers' access to the UK labour market, the ICTU
supported the introduction of temporary transitional measures in Ireland.
The union movements in both countries have adopted an inclusive and 'rights-
based' approach to immigration and have sought equal rights and entitlements
for migrant workers. At the same time, they have also been concerned to ensure
that migration does not lead to indigenous workers' pay and conditions being
undermined.

Trade unions in receiving countries, sometimes in close cooperation with
partner organisations in sending countries – especially in Poland – and in other
cases in cooperation with employers, are actively setting up advisory services
(going beyond working conditions) and training measures (primarily language
training) for migrant workers and thereby also trying to win migrant workers
as new members. In areas of Germany and Austria bordering on EU8 countries,

where cross border commuting plays an important role, a number of regional cooperation initiatives – especially Interregional Trade Union Councils – have been established to promote the exchange of information and provide a mechanism for promoting regional integration.[18]

In Germany, as in many other countries, migrant workers are overrepresented in the low-wage sector, which is reflected in a substantial (unadjusted) wage gap between indigenous workers and recent EU8 migrants, who earn only 75 per cent of the average native wage.[19]

Given the transitional measures, any downward wage pressure has largely come via posting of workers. Along with some other factors, inward migration and political concerns about its possible impact have contributed to considerable policy and institutional changes. In particular, the German trade union movement has changed its position and is now campaigning actively for a statutory minimum wage. Also, the posted workers law (based on the EU directive) has been used to reinvigorate the legal extension of collective bargaining outcomes to entire sectors. Despite the transitional measures, Norway saw substantial inward migration in the post-2004 period, including by posted workers not covered by the transitional measures. Initially strong wage competition led to the legal extension of collective agreements in a number of affected sectors, marking a significant change in Norwegian industrial relations.

5.6   CONCLUSION

East-West post-enlargement EU migration is a highly differentiated process with diverse implications. It includes various forms of mobility in a rapidly changing economic and regulatory environment. We have noted in particular variation in the application and timing of the transitional measures and the varying impact and timing of the economic crisis on sending and receiving countries' labour markets. The interaction between the timing of both the transitional measures and the crisis impacts is also important. Since the 2004 and 2007 enlargement waves, the push and pull factors affecting migrants have thus been subject to rapid and often contradictory changes.

The economic and wage convergence between source and target countries that characterised the initial period after accession has been interrupted by the crisis. In terms of the impact of the crisis on push and pull factors, what mattered most was how a particular country and its labour market were affected. The biggest difference was not between source and target countries but between the group of European countries severely affected by the crisis (particularly the

Baltic countries, Spain and Ireland) and another group (for example, Germany and Poland) that has been much less affected.

It is evident that intra-EU labour mobility reacts more strongly to changes in the regulatory and macroeconomic environment than was the case with previous migration waves. The shock of the crisis was not just a general test of labour markets throughout Europe but revealed the relative position of migrants within those markets. Although both target and source country labour markets have varied in their performance, migrant workers were more severely affected, with (short-term) migrant labour acting as a buffer in most target countries.

Over-education is a clear phenomenon for EU10 migrants, and has a number of explanations. EU10 migrants characteristically have higher educational attainment than non-EU migrants, and in many cases higher than the local population in the target countries. This is a new phenomenon in migration history. The jobs-skills mismatch and the resulting underutilisation of human capital highlighted by our results point to one of the biggest challenges facing intra-EU labour mobility in recent years. Labour mobility in post-enlargement Europe is still relatively new, but it is worrisome that we see little sign of the associated waste of human resources and inefficient cross-border labour allocation declining as migration duration increases. This phenomenon can also be seen as a failure of migration-related policies to improve the efficiency of cross-border labour mobility. As far as single policy elements are concerned, the implications of the transitional measures are controversial at the very least. Whereas they contributed to a quantitative geographical shift of East-West migration flows that appears to be continuing after their lifting (possible network effects), they were not able to improve labour allocation, especially in the sense of tackling the underutilisation of migrant labour. At the same time, the transitional measures also contributed to qualitative divergence in terms of working conditions, with higher rates of own-account (and potentially bogus) self-employment being observed in countries that applied the transitional measures.

NOTES

1   This chapter is based on findings published in two volumes edited by the authors (Galgóczi, Leschke and Watt 2009 and 2012).

2   Cyprus and Malta also joined the EU in May 2004, but limitations on the free movement of labour do not apply to them. When we use EU10 in the following we mean both the Central and Eastern European countries (EU8) and Bulgaria and Romania (EU2).

3   The countries that still had transitional measures in place with regard to Bulgaria and Romania at the end of April 2011 were Belgium, Germany, Ireland, France, Italy, Luxembourg, Malta, the Netherlands, Austria, the United Kingdom and Spain (reintroduced in July 2011) (compare: http://ec.europa.eu/social/main. jsp?catId=466&langId=en).

4   Transitional measures do not apply to those Romanian workers and their families already employed or registered as job-seekers in Spain (European Commission 12 August 2011).

5   The year 2005 may indeed have seen the largest ever labour immigration recorded in the UK, most of it from Eastern Europe. The inflow far exceeded the UK government's estimates of the number of accession-country workers who would look for work in the UK.

6   Throughout the statistical analysis we defined migration status by the nationality of the migrant worker. Migrant workers from Malta and Cyprus are included in the EU8 and EU10 figures but their numbers are negligible.

7   An illustrative example with regard to the importance of the labour market situation is the difference in migration inflows to Nordic countries upon EU enlargement. A more favourable labour market situation and higher wages meant that Norway in particular was considerably more attractive to citizens from new EU Member States than Sweden, which was the only Nordic country that had opened its labour market fully to EU8 citizens upon enlargement (Lundborg 2009).

8   The total loss in employment between the second quarter of 2008 and the first quarter of 2011 amounted to almost seven million jobs, or 1.97 per cent of all workers and sectors in the EU15. In the same period, however, due to continuous inflows of EU10 workers, the share of EU10 workers within EU15 total employment rose from 1.33 to 1.71 per cent. Thus, while EU10 workers were more affected than nationals in terms of decreasing employment and increasing unemployment, continuing EU10 migration inflow meant that EU10 employment in EU15 labour markets grew in absolute terms at a time when EU15 labour markets shrank and employment of nationals decreased.

9   Even when considering the possible effect of the EU institutions.

10   For service mobility in the Nordic countries, compare Dølvik and Eldring (2008: 36–49); for Germany and Austria, compare Krings (2009); and for Germany, compare Fellmer and Kolb (2009).

11   The legislative proposals as well as background studies on the posting of workers can be found at http://ec.europa.eu/social/main.jsp?catId=471.

12   Data limitations, a recurrent issue with regard to migrant workers, must be emphasised here. Certain categories of workers, such as short-term seasonal workers, are unlikely to be picked up by labour force surveys (for a discussion of data limitations, see Galgóczi et al. 2012, pp. 38-40).

13   The discrepancy between the findings for shares of employees and self-employed without employees is explained by the higher proportion of nationals that are self-employed while employing workers of their own.

14   Figures for both countries are only available for 2011. No figures are available for EU8 migrants in the Netherlands.

15   By 2011, Belgium had removed its EU8 transitional measures.

16   For country case studies on Germany, Austria, the UK and Sweden, see Galgóczi, Leschke and Watt (2009a).

17   Information in this paragraph reflects the findings of Heyes and Hyland (2012).

18   For further information on cross-border commuting, including education-job mismatch, see Huber (2012).

19   Findings in this paragraph are taken from Eldring and Schulten (2012), who look at migrant workers and wage-setting institutions in four countries.

REFERENCES

Bettin, G. (2012) 'Migration from the Accession Countries to the United Kingdom and Italy: Socio-economic Characteristics, Skills Composition and Labour Market Outcomes' in B. Galgóczi, J. Leschke and A. Watt (eds.) *Migration and Labour Markets in Troubled Times: Skills Mismatch, Return Migration and Policy Responses*, Aldershot: Ashgate.

Brücker, A. and W. Warneck (2010) *Viking - Laval - Rüffert: Consequences and Policy Perspectives*, Brussels: ETUI.

Cremers, J. (2011) *In Search of Cheap Labour in Europe - Working and Living Conditions of Posted Workers*, CLR Studies 6, Amsterdam.

Dølvik, J-E. and L. Eldring (2008) *Mobility of Labour from New eu States to the Nordic Region – Development Trends and Consequences*, Copenhagen: Nordic Council of Ministers.

Eldring, L. and T. Schulten (2012) 'Migrant Workers and Wage-Setting Institutions: Experiences from Germany, Norway, Switzerland and the United Kingdom' in B. Galgóczi, J. Leschke and A. Watt (eds.) *Migration and Labour Markets in Troubled Times: Skills Mismatch, Return Migration and Policy Responses*, Aldershot: Ashgate.

European Labour Force Survey, online database: http://epp.eurostat.ec.europa.eu/portal/page/portal/labour_market/introduction.

European Commission (2006) 'Communication from the Commission to the Council, the European Parliament, the European Economic and Social Committee and the Committee of the Regions', *Report on the functioning of the transitional arrangements set out in the 2003 Accession Treaty* (period 1 May 2004–30 April 2006), COM(2006) 48 final, Brussels.

European Integration Consortium (2009) *Labour Mobility within the eu in the Context of Enlargement and the Functioning of the Transitional Arrangements*, Nuremberg.

Fellmer, S. and H. Kolb (2009) 'EU Labour Migration: Government and Social Partner Policies in Germany' in B. Galgóczi, J. Leschke and A. Watt (eds.) *EU Labour Migration since Enlargement: Trends, Impacts and Policies*, Aldershot: Ashgate.

Fihel, A. and M. Okólski (2009) 'Dimensions and Effects of Labour Migration to EU Countries: the Case of Poland' in B. Galgóczi, J. Leschke and A. Watt (eds.) *EU Labour Migration since Enlargement: Trends, Impacts and Policies*, Aldershot: Ashgate.

Fihel, A. and M. Anacka (2012) 'Return Migration to Poland in the Post-Accession Period' in B. Galgóczi, J. Leschke and A. Watt (eds.) *Migration and Labour Markets in Troubled Times: Skills Mismatch, Return Migration and Policy Responses*, Aldershot: Ashgate.

Galgóczi, B., J. Leschke and A. Watt (eds.) (2009a) *EU Labour Migration since Enlargement: Trends, Impacts and Policies*, Aldershot: Ashgate.

Galgóczi, B., J. Leschke and A. Watt (eds.) (2009b) 'Intra-EU Labour Migration: Flows, Effects and Policy Responses', *ETUI Working Paper 2009.3*, update spring 2011, ETUI: Brussels.

Galgóczi, B., J. Leschke and A. Watt (eds.) (2012) *Migration and Labour Markets in Troubled Times: Skills Mismatch, Return Migration and Policy Responses*, Aldershot: Ashgate.

Heinz, F. and M. Ward-Warmedinger (2006) 'Cross-border Labour Mobility within an Enlarged EU', *ECB Occasional Paper Series 52*.

Heyes J. and M. Hyland (2012) 'Supporting, Recruiting and Organising Migrant Workers in Ireland and the United Kingdom: A Review of Trade Union Practices' in B. Galgóczi, J. Leschke and A. Watt (eds.) *Migration and Labour Markets in Troubled Times: Skills Mismatch, Return Migration and Policy Responses*, Aldershot: Ashgate.

Holland, D., T. Fic, A. Rincon-Aznar, L. Stokes and P. Paluchowski (2011) 'Labour Mobility within the EU - The Impact of Enlargement and the Functioning of the Transitional Arrangements', Final Report, commissioned by DG Employment, Social Affairs and Inclusion.

Huber, P. (2012) 'Educational Attainment and Education–Job Mismatch of Crossborder Commuters in the EU' in B. Galgóczi, J. Leschke and A. Watt (eds.) *Migration and Labour Markets in Troubled Times: Skills Mismatch, Return Migration and Policy Responses*, Aldershot: Ashgate.

Kahanec, M. and F. Zimmermann (2010) *EU Labour Markets after Post-Enlargement Migration*, Berlin/Heidelberg: Springer.

Krings, T. (2009) 'A Race to the Bottom? Trade Unions, EU Enlargement and the Free Movement of Labour', *European Journal of Industrial Relations* 15, 1: 49–69.

Leschke, J. and A. Watt (2010) 'How do institutions affect the labour market adjustment to the economic crisis in different EU countries?', *ETUI Working Paper* 2010, ETUI: Brussels.

Lundborg, P. (2009) 'The Dimensions and Effects of EU Labour Migration in Sweden' in B. Galgóczi, J. Leschke and A. Watt (eds.) *EU Labour Migration since Enlargement: Trends, Impacts and Policies*, Aldershot: Ashgate.

Sriskandarajah, D. (ed.) (2004) *EU Enlargement and Labour Migration: An IPPR Factfile*, London: Institute for Public Policy Research.

ANNEX   A NOTE ON THE LABOUR FORCE SURVEY DATA

There is no single perfect data source that makes it possible to capture intra-EU migration movements. This is due to administrative problems with tracking and registering cross-border labour mobility but also to different, often incompatible definitions between countries.

As an alternative to population registers, the European Labour Force Survey (LFS) and its national components are widely used in research on cross-border labour mobility. Even though they have a number of limitations, they make it possible to analyse population movements and the main developments in the labour market for national and migrant workers as they use a comparable methodology in all EU countries and contain both detailed questions on employment experience and information on nationality and country of birth.

Also, the fact that they are regularly conducted and that case numbers are comparatively large render them an attractive source for research on cross-border labour mobility. As respondents are interviewed repeatedly for several quarters (rolling panel), to a limited degree the Labour Force Survey data allow for an examination of stocks of migrants at a given point in time, as well as flows. The 2008 LFS included a special module on migration with larger case numbers and more comprehensive information on the issue. The LFS also allows researchers to capture commuter migration for most countries as it contains information on place of residence and place of work.

However, a number of problems arise when comparing cross-border labour mobility and the characteristics of migrant workers between European countries. Some migration flows are not picked up by survey data; the most obvious example is undocumented work. Short-term migration (for example, seasonal employment) is also unlikely to be picked up in survey data because migrant workers who stay for only a limited period of time are usually not captured by standard survey procedures. The data constraints imply that any comparative analyses of migrant workers require cautious interpretation.

6 LABOUR MIGRATION FROM CENTRAL AND EASTERN EUROPE AND THE IMPLICATIONS FOR INTEGRATION POLICY

Godfried Engbersen

6.1 INTRODUCTION

The European Union's enlargement in 2004 and 2007 was one of the most important political innovations of the early twenty-first century. The accession of ten new Member States led to a considerable increase in labour migration. Millions of Central and Eastern Europeans went to Western Europe for work. The scale of these migration flows was unanticipated (Black et al. 2010). That was true of the migration flows to the Netherlands too. According to estimates, between 260,000 and 305,000 Central and Eastern Europeans were living in the Netherlands in 2008 (Van der Heijden et al. 2011). These estimates include Central and Eastern European labour migrants who were not registered in the Municipal Personal Records Database. Many labour migrants in fact do not register, even though they live and work in the Netherlands. These undocumented people can make it very difficult for local councils because they have no idea how many Central and Eastern Europeans reside within their boundaries, or who they are.

I wish to emphasise from the outset that labour migration today takes place in an entirely different institutional context than the guest worker migration of the 1960s and 1970s. Unlike today's EU labour migrants, Moroccan and Turkish guest workers did not have the option of 'commuting' after the borders closed in 1973 (Engbersen 2012a). As a result, large numbers of Turks and Moroccans settled permanently in Western Europe, including the Netherlands (Sassen 1999). The Dutch welfare state has also undergone fundamental changes in recent years. Access to social welfare schemes has become more selective, and national assistance benefits are now a local matter. Only people who have put down local roots have access to national assistance or other local social safety nets ('residence criterion' or 'ties with the region').

The public housing sector was privatised in the early 1990s, and labour migrants are now considered responsible for their own housing. Employers have nothing more than a 'moral obligation' in that respect (Tweede Kamer 2010-2011, 29 407, no. 116). Another institutional change is that labour migration policy is more selective and more differentiated than it used to be. One example is that Romanians and Bulgarians will remain subject to the transitional measures until January 2014, which require them to have a work permit to work in the Netherlands. Polish workers have had free access to the Dutch labour market since May 2007. Nevertheless, Bulgarians and Romanians still travel to the Netherlands without work permits and become active in local informal economies (Snel et al. 2010). The final institutional change is that the Netherlands' integration policy is now based more firmly on the premise that migrants are responsible for themselves and that they have an obligation to contribute to Dutch society as 'active citizens' (Schinkel and Van Houdt 2010). All these changes have led to a fragmentation of the Netherlands' current labour migration and integration policy.

In this essay, I address two questions. The first is: what is the *nature* of labour migration from Central and Eastern Europe? Are migrants here temporarily or do they 'commute', i.e. return to their country of origin after each 'tour of duty'? Or are they settling here permanently, the way the Turkish and Moroccan guest workers did? Second: what are the implications of the new labour migration for *today's integration policy*? Like other EU Member States, the Netherlands has so far focused on the integration of non-EU migrants. EU citizens have the right to move freely throughout the Union; this is referred to as 'mobility' rather than 'migration'. The new labour migration makes an interesting case study, as it reveals the implications for local authorities of decisions taken at higher policymaking levels (Europe, the national government).

I begin with an historical sketch of labour migration based on Thomas and Znaniecki's classic study *The Polish Peasant* (1918-1922). I then present a typology of contemporary labour migration and discuss some of the social problems associated with the new labour migration. Finally, I look at the challenges for integration policy. I base my assessment on the outcomes of the Dutch study *Arbeidsmigratie in vieren* (Engbersen et al. 2011), which investigated labour migration in large, medium-sized, and small Dutch municipalities. The study, which involved conducting interviews with 654 Polish, Romanian and Bulgarian labour migrants in eleven municipalities, explored their position in society and the community and relationships between different patterns of labour migration and integration.

6.2 THE POLISH PEASANT

The first volume of a five-part series entitled *The Polish Peasant in Europe and America* was published in 1918. Written by W.I. Thomas and Florian Znaniecki, it was one of the founding classics of American sociology. One important source for the two authors was a series of letters – the 'peasant letters' – that Polish migrants in the US had received from their relatives back home.

The story goes that Thomas came across the letters by accident during a visit to a Polish neighbourhood in Chicago. They had been tossed out of a window and happened to land at his feet (Collins and Makowski 2005). In *The Polish Peasant*, Thomas and Znaniecki analysed the letters in order to investigate the relationship between the old and the new world and the social changes taking place in Poland and the United States. The Polish Peasant is therefore regarded as the first serious 'transnational' study, long before transnationalism became a concept in migration and integration studies (for an overview, see Vertovec 2009).

In *The Polish Peasant*, Thomas and Znaniecki describe two interrelated processes to explain the integration of Poles in the United States: 'social disorganisation' and 'social reorganisation'. The first refers to their observation that the rules of traditional Polish institutions (rooted in traditional agrarian, family and religious ties) no longer functioned in the new world. Thomas and Znaniecki (1984: 191) defined social disorganisation as "a decrease of the influence of existing social rules of behaviour upon individual members of the group". Social reorganisation, on the other hand, was the process whereby these institutions were adapted to the new circumstances in the US. Thomas and Znaniecki also described how new institutions that emerged from the process of social reorganisation played an important role in integrating Polish immigrants into American society. Their study led to a more nuanced view of the integration process.

> "...'assimilation' is not an individual but a group phenomenon..., the creation of a society which in structure and attitudes is neither Polish nor American but constitutes a specific new product whose raw materials have been partly drawn from Polish traditions, partly from the new conditions in which the immigrants live, and partly from American values as the immigrant sees and interprets them. It is this Polish-American society, not American society, that constitutes the social milieu into which the immigrant from Poland becomes incorporated and to whose standards and institutions he must adapt himself" (Thomas and Znaniecki 1984: 240).

One of the main themes of *The Polish Peasant* concerns the negative impacts of social disorganisation, for example crime and other forms of deviant behaviour. This radical sociological perspective – that social change leads to a decline in social control and may contribute to crime – laid the foundations for the development of American criminology. It is a perspective that is still relevant today.

At the time that Thomas and Znaniecki were writing *The Polish Peasant*, more than two million Poles had immigrated to the United States. It was later described as a period of exceptional mobility, for example by Moch in her historical study Moving Europeans (1992). In her analysis of three centuries of migration, she identifies four separate periods: pre-industrial Europe (1650-1750); the early industrial era (1750-1815); the age of urbanisation and industrialisation (1815-1914); and the twentieth century (1914-1990). In identifying these periods, she also describes four migration systems that perpetuate themselves. The first system is that of 'local migration', with mobility taking place within local labour, property and marriage markets. The second is 'circular migration', with migrants returning home after a certain period (e.g. after the harvest). The third is 'chain migration'. This is when settled migrants send for their families or help migrants who wish to settle in the same town or city. The final system is 'career migration', in which the requirements of new employers (e.g. ecclesiastical organisations or governments) eclipse the needs and wishes of local communities. These institutions impose the time of migration and the destination (for example church officials or school staff).

The dominant system in the pre-industrial era was local migration. Chain migration became more significant in the age of early industrialisation, with people settling in the emerging, expanding cities. Local migration declined in importance in the nineteenth century, with a shift towards chain migration and career migration over increasingly longer distances. Migrants even crossed the Atlantic.

> "In the end, the men, women, and children who took to the road produced a very different population in 1914 than a century earlier. This was a free, urbanized, and proletarian population. Legally free to move, a decreasing proportion of people were kept in place, or even in the countryside, by land ownership. By the end of the century, the boom in city-building had slacked and work in Metallurgy and mining became more steady. The combined result of these two trends was to give more people permanent work at the expense of seasonal employment, and a greater proportion of workers were constrained neither by possessions nor by the law to stay in place. The labor force in western Europe was an international one, in which Belgians, Italians, Irish, and Poles in particular worked across an international boundary – if not across the Atlantic – from home" (Moch 1992: 160).

The mobile nineteenth century was followed by a century in which the rise of national states and two world wars made it increasingly crucial to control migration flows. After the Second World War, national states progressively monopolised the legitimate tools for regulating mobility (Torpey 1998). Examples are the active recruitment by Western European governments of 'guest workers' in the 1960s and the restrictive migration policy intended to prevent undesirable migrants from the 1980s onward ('Fortress Europe').

The European Union underwent a major expansion at the start of the twenty-first century, giving Central and Eastern Europeans the right to move freely throughout the EU. The Western European Member States also opened their labour markets to the new EU citizens, some of them immediately and others later (Holland et al. 2011). As a result, millions of Poles and other labour migrants from Central and Eastern Europe (mainly Romanians and Bulgarians) sought work in Western Europe. They first went to the United Kingdom, Ireland, Sweden and Norway, and then to the Netherlands and other countries. In January 2008, Poland's national statistics office estimated that 2.3 million Poles were at work in Western Europe (Friberg 2012). What are these patterns of labour migration, and how do they differ from the migration systems described by Moch?

6.3   LABOUR MIGRATION IN FOURS

Like the mobile nineteenth century, today's labour migration from Central and Eastern Europe can be described in terms of its diversity. That diversity is reflected in four dominant patterns of labour migration (see Engbersen et al. 2011). These patterns – which have also been documented in ethnographic studies and small-scale ethno-surveys – closely resemble Moch's migration systems (Eade et al. 2006; Düvell and Vogel 2006; Grabowska-Lusinska and Okolski 2009). Because the new labour migration is of such recent origin, however, it is too soon to refer to them as 'migration systems'. The four patterns are derived from two dimensions of migration and integration, i.e. (1) the degree of the labour migrants' attachment to their destination country; and (2) the degree of their attachment to their home country. These attachments can be 'weak' or 'strong' (see Figure 6.1), and the four patterns can also be consecutive.[1] Temporary migration can lead to transnational and ultimately to settlement migration, but this process does not apply for every individual labour migrant (Friberg 2012). Contemporary labour migration is not only diverse, but also dynamic and changeable (Engbersen 2012a).

The Dutch study entitled *Arbeidsmigratie in vieren* (Labour migration in fours) shows that labour migrants who conform to the pattern of *temporary, circular migration* do not mix much with the local population. They speak only a few words of Dutch and are mainly interested in earning money that they can invest in their country of origin. They send about 5400 Euros home every year, on average. Many have partners and children in their country of origin. They often do seasonal work in agriculture or horticulture, but may also be skilled craftsmen.

The pattern of *transnational or binational migration* concerns migrants who have integrated in the Netherlands but maintain close ties with their own country. They have a lot of contact with the local population, relatively speaking (they also speak Dutch), but also maintain their relationships in their country of origin. They send quite a lot of money back home (about 3900 Euros on average). This pattern is common among highly skilled migrants and, to a lesser extent, among those with secondary school qualifications. They tend to work in semi-skilled occupations and earn a decent income. They have often been in the Netherlands for a longer period of time and have a partner here, but no children (yet). They expect to return to their home country eventually, or migrate to another country.

The pattern of *settlement migration* is mainly found among highly skilled migrants who have been in the Netherlands for a long time and who indicated during interviews that they wished to stay for more than five years. This group sends a relatively small amount of money back home (about 700 Euros on average). They tend to have had children in the Netherlands and their partner does not live (or no longer lives) in their country of origin. They often work in relatively high-skilled occupations.

Footloose migration can be found mainly among migrants who have only been in the Netherlands for a relatively short period of time. They have few roots in Dutch society, speak very poor Dutch, have no Dutch friends and insecure jobs (many of them do not have work permits). But they also have little contact with their home country and send almost no money back home. Most of them, though not all, have had little schooling. A relatively large number of footloose migrants are single and are fairly young when they come to the Netherlands. That also explains why they feel little attachment to their home country. They have few family obligations. Like the 'stayers', they send very little money home, about 800 Euros on average.

In addition to the lower cost of travel, three factors are responsible for the diverse nature of contemporary migration patterns. The first is the elimination of internal borders within the enlarged EU, making it easier for people to travel back and forth.

The second factor is how the urban and rural labour markets operate. There is a permanent demand for cheap, temporary, flexible labour. Favell (2008) believes that Eastern Europeans are the new proletariat of Western European labour markets. The EU's enlargement has led to a new hierarchy in the labour market, with workers from Central and Eastern Europe tending to take marginal and insecure jobs. That marginalism explains the patterns of return and circular migration. Only migrants who carve out a stable position for themselves in the labour market will remain. Others take advantage of the huge wage differences between the Netherlands and their own country, leading to their rational choice to spend most of the money they have earned at home.

Figure 6.1   Patterns of labour migration from Central and Eastern Europe after EU enlargement in May 2004 and January 2007

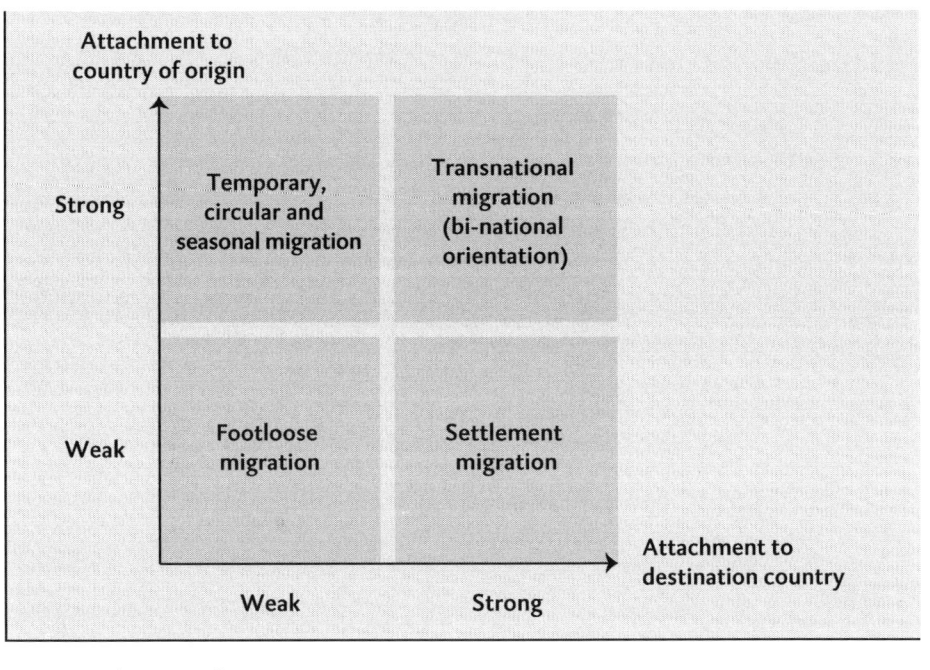

Source: Engbersen et al. 2011.

The third factor is the process of individualisation in family relationships in Central and Eastern Europe (Ornacka and Szczepaniak-Wiecha 2005), which has resulted in many young people being freer to move about and travel to the West without family obligations. The family as the 'engine of immigration' (Massey and Philips 1999) has become less important in East-West migration. One striking finding in the Dutch study was that half of the respondents do not send money home to their families. Tilly's assertion (1990) that it is not 'individuals' but 'networks' that migrate does not apply to East-West migration, in any event.

The various migration patterns identified above are linked to *varying forms and grades of integration*. As in *The Polish Peasant*, a proportion of the migrants in the Dutch study showed signs of assimilation: a waning attachment to the migrant's own country and a growing focus on Dutch society. Nevertheless, even this group maintained its contacts with Poland. Settlement migrants have an average of 76 contacts a month with friends and family in their country of origin (Engbersen et al. 2011). There is also the notable presence of Polish institutions developed in the Netherlands, such as weekend schools, churches, newspapers and shops. They exist only because there is a large enough Polish population (temporary or permanent) to support them.

Alongside this traditional settlement process, other forms of integration can be observed. Some groups (especially the circular migrants) are mainly transients and commuters who only integrate to a certain extent owing to the temporary nature of their jobs. They make use of flexible facilities, such as 'Polish hotels', campgrounds and private boarding houses, and are to some extent dependent on rack-renters and unscrupulous employment agencies. Other migrants integrate economically, socially and culturally, but remain focused on their country of origin. They expect to return to their home country eventually, or migrate to another country. This pattern confirms earlier findings that transnationalism need not be at the expense of successful integration (Snel et al. 2006; Vertovec 2009). Those who integrate successfully into Dutch society also have more financial scope to operate transnationally. The final group is relatively rootless. They feel little attachment either to the Netherlands or to their home country. Some of them are part of a relatively mobile 'underclass' that has trouble finding work and housing (Snel et al. 2010). One example is the Turkish-speaking Bulgarians, who often try their luck in the Netherlands without possessing a work permit. They feel little attachment to their home country and rely heavily on informal Turkish circles in the Netherlands.

6.4   LOCAL SOCIAL PROBLEMS

Some of the new labour migrants integrate smoothly into Dutch society. That is mainly the case for those who fall into the category of transnational or settlement migrants. Nevertheless, social problems have arisen that are associated mainly with the other two types of labour migration. They involve such matters as *non-registration, irregular work* (moonlighting, unscrupulous employment agencies), *irregular and poor housing* (spatial concentrations, overcrowding, exploitation, poor quality, homelessness), *quality of life* (deviant behaviour on the street and in neighbourhoods), *assimilation* (how to arrange this for EU citizens?) and *schooling* (labour migrants' children enrolling and withdrawing from schools, truancy). There are also *crime-related* problems. Police statistics in The Hague and Rotterdam show that Poles and Romanians tend to be involved in certain types of crime, such as shoplifting and acts of violence towards one another (Snel et al. 2011; Engbersen 2012b).

Thomas and Znaniecki's 'social disorganisation' theory is still relevant. Labour migration may be accompanied by a waning level of social control in the migrant's own circle, influenced by the loose, temporary attachments of what is largely a male group. The final problem is a possible *dependence on benefits* (in particular national assistance). If too many Central and Eastern Europeans claim national assistance benefits, local budgets may come under pressure.

What is typical of almost all social problems is that they are felt most keenly at local level. That is especially true of the problems associated with crime, housing, quality of life, education and registration. The problems of homelessness and dependence on national assistance appear to be limited.[2] The most elementary issues concern the nature and scale of labour migration and the demands it makes on housing and local public facilities (such as education). For local policymakers to be able to develop a rational policy, they need to understand the scale, diversity and dynamics of labour migration. Local authorities furthermore depend heavily on private and semi-private parties when developing that policy (such as property developers and housing corporations aiming to build housing for migrant groups). Local social problems show how arbitrary the distinction is between 'integration policy' for non-EU migrants and the 'free movement policy' for EU labour migrants. EU labour migrants may also need to learn the language and become familiar with Dutch society, even if they remain in the Netherlands for only a short time. The government's policy does not oblige this category of migrants to assimilate, however. Nevertheless, in recent years eu citizens were able to take part in subsidised, locally organised assimilation programmes, on a voluntary basis. Between 2007 and 2012, 270 local Dutch authorities ran 183,000 assimilation programmes. Some 17,000 EU labour migrants took part in these programmes.[3] That will no longer be possible, however, because funding has been slashed and the basic premise of integration policy now is that migrants are responsible for their own assimilation.

6.5   TOWARDS A MORE DIFFERENTIATED INTEGRATION POLICY

Anyone scrutinising EU labour migration policy will be struck by the lack of a measured integration policy. EU *policy* is based on the *free movement* of persons and support for labour migration. Dutch *national policy* is mainly concerned with the negative sides of labour migration; it is also dominated by the fear of large-scale *settlement migration* flows of Eastern and Central Europeans who could eventually claim social welfare benefits.[4] *Local policy*, finally, is generally *improvised* depending on the type of labour migration involved. And yet, it is at local level that the most innovative policy has been implemented. The local authorities of Westland, for example, are working with employers and actively approaching labour migrants in order to ensure their registration in the municipality. The City of The Hague is actively seeking partnership with labour migrants' own organisations.

But there are limits to what local authorities can and are permitted to do. That is why they have been making specific efforts to influence national policy, ever since the first 'Poles Summit' in 2007.[5] Since 2010, their efforts have induced the national government to consult the local authorities of The Hague, Rot-

terdam, Westland, Medemblik, Utrecht, Schiedam, Amsterdam and Eindhoven. The national government has also set up five working groups focusing
on (i) registration and information; (ii) housing; (iii) integration and language;
(iv) remigration, and (v) work. Local authorities and other stakeholders (migrants' own organisations, employment agencies, housing providers) participate in the working groups, which discuss a wide range of topics that are
subsequently covered in official letters addressed to Parliament concerning
EU migration measures.[6] Many of these measures focus on tightening up
enforcement and registration policy and emphasising the labour migrants'
own responsibility towards making his or her stay in the Netherlands a success.
Many are also meant to assist local authorities and inspection services in effectively combating irregular housing and employment practices and dependency
on benefits.

Local initiatives provide a good indication of what should be done. A differentiated policy is needed that takes the four patterns of migration and their mutual
relationship into account. At this point in time, public debate and policymaking
at certain levels tend to focus on only one of the four patterns, specifically
either temporary migration or settlement migration. The EU is concerned
about mobility, whereas national government emphasises the repercussions
of settlement. The reality, however, is that the four patterns are *parallel* and
simultaneous. The four types could be used as a guideline for a differentiated
policy tailored to local needs.

To support a differentiated policy of this kind, the authorities should meet
three requirements:
1   They should give labour migrants *useful information* (both in their coun-
     try of origin and in their destination country) about their employment
     and legal position, including housing, education and health care. They
     can do so on European and national websites that provide information
     in the migrants' own language, or through local helpdesks (cf. the expat
     desks) (Van Bochove et al. 2011).
2   They should develop a satisfactory system of *registration* so that they
     have a better understanding of the nature of migration patterns and pos-
     sible fluctuations between the various patterns. For example, is tempo-
     rary migration increasing or decreasing?
3   There should be effective *legislation* (and enforcement mechanisms) for
     tackling unscrupulous housing providers, employment agencies and
     employers. Efforts should also be made to combat the abuse of certain
     legal loopholes allowing migrants to work in the Netherlands as 'self-
     employed' or 'posted workers'.

In addition to these requirements, the authorities should work towards achieving the following four objectives:

1   A flexible infrastructure for incorporating *temporary, circular labour migrants* into Dutch society. Adequate housing is essential in this respect. All sorts of improvised solutions have been attempted in recent years to organise housing for this group, from campgrounds to housing estates awaiting approval for demolition. In addition, migrant 'hotels' have been founded in various municipalities. There is an urgent need for inexpensive, simple but decent housing that affords the residents privacy. The challenge is to make this sort of housing available. Both private parties and housing corporations have a role to play. Cities such as The Hague and Rotterdam are more likely to need housing for settlement or transnational migrants than the rural municipalities. Another option is to make housing *arrangements* at regional level so that the responsibility for providing housing is shared. In the event of long-term problems, it is up to local authorities to take the lead in finding solutions, in consultation with employers, employment agencies, and housing corporations. That is also true of problems that arise once the migrants' employment has ended. Workers should not be thrown out of their homes as soon as their contracts are terminated.

2   Mechanisms for assimilating labour migrants who wish to remain in the Netherlands for a longer period of time (*transnational and settlement migrants*). The *Arbeidsmigratie in vieren* study showed that some of the 'stayers' had taken courses in Dutch offered by commercial providers. They had paid for the lessons themselves. Figures provided by the Dutch Ministry of the Interior and Kingdom Relations also show that labour migrants made use of facilities for voluntary assimilation. To provide even more support for assimilation, the authorities would do well to develop e-learning products so that migrants can teach themselves the language. They can also encourage employers to arrange language courses for their employees. But we should accept that proficiency in Dutch is not top priority for labour migrants who only intend staying in the Netherlands for a short time. Transnational and settlement migrants are likely to benefit the most from knowing Dutch. The authorities should also be concerned about *educating* the children of EU labour migrants (lateral entry into the Dutch education system). Many EU labour migrants live in multicultural neighbourhoods in the cities. Extra efforts are needed to ensure that their children find their place in primary education.

3   Mechanisms for tackling the social problems arising from *footloose migration* (cf. Snel et al. 2011). These are problems of crime, unemployment, irregular work, homelessness and addiction. More information is further needed about the possibility of remigration for migrants who have no means of support in the Netherlands. Free movement within the borders

of the EU is one of the fundamental rights of EU citizens. However, that
right is based on the idea that residents from other EU Member States
will support themselves (at least until they have worked long enough
to gain access to social welfare schemes). National and local authorities
should investigate the possibility of remigration and develop practical
rules in that regard. Local government can work with civil society and
migrant organisations to assist in the voluntary return of homeless
migrants who are unable to find work or support themselves in the
Netherlands.

4   Incorporation of EU labour migration into current knowledge migration
policy. Some of the *highly skilled transnational and settlement migrants*
can be covered under the national knowledge migration policy and
local expat policy. This would involve retaining Polish, Bulgarian and
Romanian skilled professionals for the Dutch knowledge economy on the
one hand, and supporting their integration into Dutch urban society on
the other. The expat policy developed by the City of The Hague can serve
as an example (Van Bochove et al. 2011).

6.6   CONCLUSION

The growing internal mobility in the EU is differentiated in nature. There are
different patterns of labour migration characterised either by transience (short
and medium term) or settlement. These patterns not only have economic implications but also social repercussions for cities and regions. The influx of
Central and Eastern Europeans has become an important policy issue in the receiving towns and cities, not only in the Netherlands but elsewhere in Europe.
One example is the problem of homelessness and antisocial behaviour (Crellen
2010; Garapich 2011; Mostowska 2011). The policy arrangements made at local
level are an attempt to regulate the multiple patterns of contemporary labour
migration. Those arrangements emphasise and prioritise such issues as registration, housing, illegal employment agencies, remigration policy and assimilation. But the power of local authorities is restricted on many fronts by eu and
national legislation (Puymbroeck et al. 2011; Engbersen and Snel 2012).

The fact that there are local arrangements at all indicates that the current distinction between 'mobility policy' for EU labour migrants and 'integration
policy' for non-EU migrants is an artificial one that fails to consider that different groups of labour migrants basically need help during their temporary, me-
dium- or long-term stay in the Netherlands. They need adequate *information*
(for example they ought to know their rights and be familiar with key Dutch
institutions) and access to *decent housing* that suits their intended length of
stay and career plans. Local governments struggling with the consequences of

new labour migration also require more official forms of integration policy. In the first place, that means providing housing (and to some extent educational facilities); it also means regulating and preventing social problems such as homelessness and crime. The fact that EU labour migration is 'permanently temporary' in nature makes a review of traditional integration policy necessary. Because EU labour migrants are involved, the current remigration policy must also be reconsidered. Anyone studying the assimilation of labour migrants in Dutch society will furthermore see that many of them have in fact managed to carve out a place for themselves on their own – entirely in line with current integration ideology.

NOTES

1   The four patterns of labour migration are not visible to the same extent. Research
        by Van der Heijden et al. (2011) made it possible to use a specific weighting factor
        for our population, with non-registered respondents being assigned more weight,
        so that, after weighting, our registration density corresponds with the registration
        density among Poles, Bulgarians and Romanians in the Netherlands estimated by
        Van der Heijden et al. (2011). According to subsequent analysis, 23% of the Bulgarian,
        Romanian and Polish labour migrants follow the pattern of circular migration, 13%
        the pattern of transnational migration, 22% the pattern of settlement migration, and
        41% the pattern of footloose migration.

2   Two observations from Rotterdam illustrate this. In Rotterdam, overnight shelters
        for homeless persons are restricted to those who satisfy the criterion of 'ties with
        the region'. Most Central and Eastern European homeless persons do not satisfy this
        criterion. According the city's figures, seven homeless persons from Central and
        Eastern Europe were permitted to use the overnight shelter in 2010. In winter, how-
        ever, a special arrangement goes into effect in extremely cold temperatures. Extra
        capacity is made available, and there are no restrictions. In the winter of 2010/2011,
        the winter arrangement was in effect in Rotterdam for 46 days. In this period, 59 per-
        sons from Central and Eastern Europe made use of an overnight shelter (Engbersen
        et al. 2011). The City of Rotterdam's most recent analysis of its EU labour migrants
        programme reports that only one person from Central and Eastern Europe was ad-
        mitted to long-term homeless accommodation between 1 January and 31 December
        2011. Central and Eastern Europeans also make only modest claims on national assis-
        tance. In January 2012, Rotterdam had 106 Central and Eastern Europeans receiving
        national assistance benefits (out of a total population of between 26,000 and 34,000
        Central and Eastern Europeans).

3   These figures were provided by the Ministry of the Interior.

4   The Netherlands has submitted proposals to the EU to amend Directive 2004/38,
        concerning the free movement of persons. According to the directive, someone who
        has worked in a host country for more than a year and becomes involuntarily unem-
        ployed is entitled to remain in that country for an indefinite period of time. That can
        easily lead to a right to claim national assistance. The Dutch Government wants to
        amend the directive so that an EU citizen only acquires the right to remain in the
        Netherlands indefinitely after he or she has worked there for more than five years.

5   Since the first 'Poles Summit' in Rotterdam in 2007, Dutch local authorities have
        confronted the national government with local problems arising from Central and
        Eastern European labour migration.

6   See Tweede Kamer, 2010-2011, 29 407, no. 116 *Maatregelen arbeidsmigratie uit
        Midden- en Oost-Europa*; and Tweede Kamer 2011-2012, 29407, no. 130 *Arbeids-
        migratie uit EU-landen*.

REFERENCES

Black, R., G. Engbersen, M. Okolski and C. Pantiru (eds.) (2010) *A Continent Moving West? EU Enlargement and Labour Migration from Central and Eastern Europe*, Amsterdam: Amsterdam University Press.

Bochove, M. van, K. Rusinovic and G. Engbersen (2011) *On the Red Carpet. Expats in Rotterdam and The Hague*, Rotterdam: Erasmus University (Report) http://repub.eur.nl/res/pub/33097/metis_176261.pdf.

Crellen, J. (2010) 'Sharing Solutions; How Can We Support Central and Eastern Europeans who Become Homeless in the UK'?, pp. 16-18 in *Homeless in Europe. Homelessness and migration in Europe*, The Magazine of FEANTSA (Summer).

Düvell F. and D. Vogel (2006) 'Polish Migrants: Tensions between Sociological Typologies and State Categories', pp. 267-289 in A. Triandafyllidou (eds.) *Contemporary Polish Migration in Europe. Complex Patterns of Movement and Settlement*, Lewiston, NY: Edwin Mellen Press.

Eade J., S. Drinkwater and M. Garapich (2006) *Class and Ethnicity: Polish Migrants in London*, Guildford: University of Surrey.

Engbersen, G. (2012a) 'Migration Transitions in an Era of Liquid Migration. Reflections on Fassmann and Reeger', pp. 91-105 in M. Okolski (ed.) *Europe: The Continent of Immigrants: Trends, Structures and Policy Implications*, Amsterdam: Amsterdam University Press.

Engbersen, G. (2012b) MOE-*landers in Rotterdam: aard, omvang en sociale implicaties. Een essay ten behoeve van ronde tafelsessie over nieuwe arbeidsmigratie in Rotterdam*, Gemeente Rotterdam, August 2012.

Engbersen, G. en E. Snel (2012) 'Lokaal bestuur en de uitbreiding van Europa. De bestuurlijke aanpak van de arbeidsmigratie uit Midden- en Oost-Europa', BESTUURSKUNDE 1: 25-32.

Engbersen, G., M. Ilies, A. Leerkes, E. Snel and R. van der Meij (2011) *Arbeidsmigratie in vieren. Bulgaren en Roemenen vergeleken met Polen*, Den Haag: NCIS Institute.

Favell, A. (2008) 'The New Face of East-West Migration in Europe', *Journal of Ethnic and Migration Studies* 34, 5: 735-752.

Friberg, J. H. (2012) 'The Stages of Migration. From Going abroad to Settling Down: Post-Accession Polish Workers in Norway', *Journal of Ethnic and Migration Studies* 38, 10: 1589-1605.

Garapich, M. (2011) 'Of Alcohol and Men. Survival, Masculinities and Anti-Institutionalism of Polish Homeless Men in a Global City', Migration between Poland and United Kingdom, Special issue of *Studia Migracyjne-Przeglad Polonijny* 1: 309-330.

Grabowska-Lusinska, I. and M. Okólski (2009) *Emigracja ostatnia?*, Warsaw: Wydawnictwo Naukowe Scholar.

Heijden, P.G.M. van der, M. Cruyff and G. van Gils (2011) *Aantallen geregistreerde en niet-geregistreerde burgers uit* MOE-*landen die in Nederland verblijven*, Utrecht: Universiteit Utrecht.

Holland, D., T. Fic, A. Rincon-Aznar, L. Stokes and P. Paluchowski (2011) 'Labour Mobility within the EU-The Impact of Enlargement and the Functioning of the Transnational Arrangements, Final Report, commissioned by DG Employment, Social Affairs and Inclusion.

Massey, D.S. and J.A. Philips (1999) 'Engines of Immigration: Stocks of Human and Social Capital in Mexico', *Social Science Quarterly* 81: 33-48.

Moch, L.P. (1992) *Moving Europeans: Migration in Western Europe since 1650*, Bloomington: Indiana University Press.

Mostowska, M. (2011) 'Services for Homeless Immigrants: The Social Welfare Capital of Polish Rough Sleepers in Brussels and Oslo', *European Journal of Homelessness* 5, 1: 27-47.

Ornacka, K. and I. Szczepaniak-Wiecha (2005) 'The Contemporary Family in Poland: New Trends and Phenomena', *Journal of Family and Economic Issues* 26, 2: 195-225.

Puymbroeck N. van, S. van de Pol and S. Oosterlynck (2011) 'Oost-West mobiliteit en de bestuurlijke europeanisering van steden. Een vergelijkende studie van de cases Gent en Rotterdam', *Tijdschrift voor Sociologie* 32, 3-4: 291-326.

Sassen, S. (1999) *Guests and Aliens*, New York: The New Press.

Schinkel, W. and F. van Houdt (2010) 'The double helix of cultural assimilationism and neo-liberalism: citizenship in contemporary governmentality', *The British Journal of Sociology* 61, 4: 696-715.

Snel, E. et al. (2006) 'Transnational involvement and social integrations', *Global Networks* 6, 3: 285-308.

Snel, E., J. Burgers, G. Engbersen, M. Ilies, R. van der Meij and K. Rusinovic (2010) *Arbeidsmigranten uit Bulgarije, Polen en Roemenië in Rotterdam. Sociale leefsituatie, arbeidspositie en toekomstperspectief*, Den Haag: NICIS.

Snel, E., G. Engbersen, M. Ilies, R. van der Meij and J. Hamberg (2011) *De schaduwzijden van de nieuwe arbeidsmigratie. Dakloosheid en overlast van Midden- en Oost-Europese arbeidsmigranten in Den Haag*. Rotterdam: EUR.

Thomas, W.I. and F. Znaniecki (1984) *The Polish Peasant in Europe and America: Organization and Disorganization in America*, University of Illinois Press.

Tilly, C. (1990) 'Transplanted Networks', p. 79-95 in V. Yans-McLaughlin (ed.) *Immigration Reconsidered: History, Sociology, and Politics*. New York: Oxford University Press.

Torpey, J. (1998) 'Coming and Going: on the State Monopolization of the Legitimate 'Means of Movement', *Sociological Theory* 16, 3: 239-259.

Tweede Kamer, Kamerstukken 2010-2011, 29 407, nr. 116, *Maatregelen arbeidsmigratie uit Midden- en Oost-Europa*.

Tweede Kamer, Kamerstukken 2011-2012, 29407, nr. 130, *Arbeidsmigratie uit EU-landen*.

Vertovec, S. (2009) *Transnationalism*, London en New York: Routledge.

ABOUT THE AUTHORS

Bridget Anderson is Professor of Migration and Citizenship and Deputy Director at the Centre on Migration, Policy and Society (COMPAS) in Oxford. She works on projects about citizenship and the way people come to feel at home in a place; the economics and politics of labour shortages; and the relationship between migration and the state at global, national and local level. She is particularly interested in the balance of power and inequalities based on race, gender, class and immigration status. Anderson has a DPhil in sociology and previous training in philosophy and modern languages. She is currently working on a monograph entitled *Us and Them: the Dangerous Politics of Immigration Controls.* She is the co-editor (with Martin Ruhs) of *Who Needs Migrant Workers? Labour Shortages, Immigration and Public Policy.*

Godfried Engbersen is Professor of Sociology at Erasmus University in Rotterdam and a fellow of the Royal Netherlands Academy of Arts and Sciences. His current research activities focus on irregular migration, the relationship between restrictive migration regimes and crime, local and transnational citizenship and liquid migration from Central and Eastern Europe. His latest books are *Fatale Remedies. De onbedoelde effecten van beleid en kennis* (Fatal Remedies. The Unintended Consequences of Policy and Science) (2009), *A Continent Moving West? EU Enlargement and Labour Migration from Central and Eastern Europe* (with Richard Black, Marek Okolski and Christina Pantiru) (2010) and the policy report *Arbeidsmigratie in vieren* (Labour Migration in Fours) (2011).

Béla Galgóczi has been a Senior Researcher at the European Trade Union Institute (ETUI) in Brussels since 2003. He graduated in electrical engineering and sociology from the University of Budapest. He completed postgraduate studies in political science at the University of Amsterdam and obtained a PhD in economics in Budapest. His fields of research include the free movement of capital and labour in Europe in a global context, restructuring and economic sustainability. In 2009, he co-edited *EU Labour Migration since Enlargement. Trends, Impacts and Policies* (with Janine Leschke and Andrew Watt). An updated version of this publication appeared in late 2012.

Jan Willem Holtslag has been an Advisory Member of the Scientific Council for Government Policy (WRR) since 2008. His previous position was Secretary-General at the Dutch Ministry of the Interior and Kingdom Relations and, prior to that, Director-General of Public Administration for the same Ministry. He has also worked as a consultant for the Ministry of General Affairs and served as

secretary during the formation of three Governments. Holtslag studied Politics
and Social Science at the University of Amsterdam. At the WRR, he headed the
project *Toekomst van het openbaar bestuur in zijn constitutionele setting* (Future
of Public Administration in its Constitutional Setting), which resulted in 2010
in the publication *Het gezicht van de publieke zaak. Openbaar bestuur onder
ogen* (The Face of Public Affairs. A Look at Public Administration). He now
chairs the *Heroriëntatie Europa* (Reorientation Europe) project.

Monique Kremer is a Senior Researcher at the Scientific Council for Government
Policy (WRR). She studied sociology at Utrecht University and social policy
at the University of Sussex (UK). She has worked as a researcher at the NIZW
(Netherlands Institute for Care and Welfare) and Utrecht University, where she
received her PhD for her dissertation *How Welfare States Care: Culture, Gender
and Parenting in Europe* (Amsterdam University Press 2007). At the WRR she
has worked on the reports *De verzorgingsstaat herwogen*; (Reconsidering the
Welfare State), *Identificatie met Nederland* (Identifying with the Netherlands)
and *Minder pretentie, meer ambitie* (Less Pretention, More Ambition). She is
currently involved in the *Heroriëntatie Europa* (Reorientation Europe) project.
She was also appointed to a research position at the University of Amsterdam
in 2010, where she is studying the future of the welfare state in the light of migration at the request of Stichting Instituut GAK.

Georges Lemaître is Principal Administrator of the International Migration Division,
OECD Directorate for Employment, Labour and Social Affairs in Paris. He was
educated at Cornell University (1966-1970), McGill University (1971-1974) and
the University of Paris (1975-1976). He began his career at Statistics Canada,
where he remained until 1992. He joined the staff of OECD in 1994, where he
was responsible for education (PISA assessments), labour, and demography
statistics. His interests in the labour market area include part-time work, labour
dynamics, labour force participation over the life cycle and measures of labour
force skill. Lemaître joined the international migration area at OECD in 2003,
and has since focused on issues related to the integration of immigrants, cross-
border service provision, the management of migration and the harmonisation
of migration statistics.

Janine Leschke is an Associate Professor at the Department of Business and Politics at
Copenhagen Business School. Previously she worked as a Senior Researcher at
the European Trade Union Institute (ETUI) and as a PhD candidate at the labour market policy and employment unit of Wissenschaftszentrum Berlin für
Sozialforschung. She holds a PhD in political science from the Free University
of Berlin. Her research interests encompass EU labour market, social policy and
comparative welfare state analysis. She has led a number of international net-

work projects and is member of several European advisory committees, among them the European Statistical Advisory Committee (ESAC).

Demetrios Papademetriou is President and Co-Founder of the Migration Policy Institute (MPI), a Washington-based think tank dedicated to the study of international migration. He is also President of the Migration Policy Institute Europe, a non-profit, independent research institute in Brussels that aims to promote a better understanding of migration trends and effects within Europe. Papademetriou has served as Chair of the World Economic Forum's Global Agenda Council on Migration (2009-2011), as Chair of the Migration Committee of the OECD, as Director for Immigration Policy and Research at the US Department of Labor, and as Executive Editor of the *International Migration Review*. He has published more than 250 books, articles, monographs, and research reports on migration topics and advises senior government and political party officials in more than twenty countries (including numerous European Union Member States).

Martin Ruhs is a Senior Researcher at the Centre on Migration, Policy and Society (COMPAS) and a University Lecturer in Political Economy at Oxford University. Since 2010 he has also headed the Migration Observatory, which produces independent data analyses on migration and migrants in the United Kingdom. As an economist, he specialises in the economics and politics of labour immigration, with a strong international comparative dimension. He has conducted studies of the impacts and policy implications of labour immigration in the UK, Ireland, the US, Thailand and Kuwait. His recent publications have focused on migrants in low wage jobs in the UK, employer demand for migrant labour, illegality, temporary migration programmes and migrant rights. Ruhs has provided policy analysis and advice for various national governments and international institutions, including the International Labour Organisation (ILO), the International Organisation for Migration (IOM), the Global Commission on International Migration (GCIM), the United Nations Development Programme (UNDP) and the Swedish Presidency of the European Union. He is currently a member of the Migration Advisory Committee (MAC), which advises the UK government on labour immigration policy.

Erik Schrijvers is a Senior Researcher at the Scientific Council for Government Policy (WRR). He studied at Utrecht University, taking a degree (*cum laude*) in international relations in 2002 and in the philosophy of history in 2003. He received his PhD in 2012 for his dissertation *Ongekozen bestuur. Opkomst en ondergang van het stelsel van adviescolleges en bedrijfsorganen* (1945-1995) (Unelected Government. The Rise and Fall of the System of Advisory Councils and Industrial Bodies, 1945-1995). From 2007 to 2011 he worked at

Utrecht University's Department of Political History, where he had a part-time appointment. At the WRR he has worked on the reports *Bewijzen van goede dienstverlening* (Proofs of Good Service Provision) and *Identificatie met Nederland* (Identifying with the Netherlands). He now coordinates the *Heroriëntatie Europa* (Reorientation Europe) project.